THE VOICE of SILENCE

A Rabbi's Journey into a Trappist
Monastery and Other Contemplations

Rabbi Dr.Analia Bortz, MD

WESTBOW
PRESS®
A DIVISION OF THOMAS NELSON
& ZONDERVAN

Scripture taken from the King James Version of the Bible

WestBow Press books may be ordered through booksellers or by contacting:

WestBow Press
A Division of Thomas Nelson & Zondervan
1663 Liberty Drive
Bloomington, IN 47403
www.westbowpress.com
1 (866) 928-1240

ISBN: 978-1-5127-9394-9 (sc)
ISBN: 978-1-5127-9395-6 (hc)
ISBN: 978-1-5127-9393-2 (e)

Library of Congress Control Number: 2017910921

Print information available on the last page.

WestBow Press rev. date: 08/14/2017

"The voyage of discovery lies not in seeking new horizons but in having new eyes".

Marcel Proust

To my parents, Esther & Isaac, who inspired me to live to my potential.

To my husband, Rabbi Mario Karpuj, my life partner and my journey partner.

To our daughters, Tamar & Adina, sources of strength and inspiration, who are not afraid to spread their wings and dream big.

This book is dedicated to Zachary Weinstein, who taught me, silently, how to overcome life's challenges, and without knowing it, changed my life forever.

CONTENTS

One

THE JOURNEY

I did not cast a vow of silence. Sometimes, it is God who tells us that we need a sabbatical for our voices, and since my voice is instrumental in my life and my livelihood, I decide to follow the doctor's orders and rest its activity to help it heal.

Without my voice, I feel asphyxiated, caged in the obstructive world of silence. My feelings of suffocation and exhaustion encase me as I can no longer express myself through the conduit of words. Instead, I find myself driving along Highway 20 on my way to Conyers, Georgia. I never thought I would drive this far away from home to encounter the unknown. Feelings of eagerness, excitement and anxiety accompany me on this route to the unfamiliar. Yet, I welcome the open-mindedness required on this journey of self-discovery.

Whenever I am at home in Atlanta on a Friday afternoon I listen to Israeli musician Etti Ankeri as she sings the *pyiutim* (poems) from medieval times. She often uses the lyrics of Rabbi Yehudah HaLevi, who lived in the eleventh and twelfth centuries, and whose heart ached with longing for Jerusalem. His longing transports me to a different dimension. Etti's voice and guttural accent introduce me to the spirit of Shabbat, the seventh day of the week, that cyclically showers me with its spiritual peace.

On Fridays, after a whole week of juggling with many professional and personal tasks, I am delighted to cook for those whom I love and the guests that will join us for a Shabbat meal. I set the table: an immaculate, white tablecloth; special Shabbat dishes; pristine napkins; and the special wooden plate that my daughter Adina made at summer camp to host the traditional braided bread, the *challah*. I needlepointed the *challah* cover. The *kiddush* cup, the wine glass, filled with sweetness that sanctifies the day. It is colorful and decorated with a design influenced by the work of Salvador Dali, one of my favorite painters. In the center of the table are the beautiful white roses that my husband brings me every Friday. They crown the table as it waits for the entrance of the Bride-- the Queen--Shabbat.

These are my roots. I am familiar with it. I cannot see myself anywhere else on a Friday evening but around the Shabbat table, singing the prayers and songs that connect me with my past and plans for my future while enjoying the present. I feel I am another link on the millennial chain that bonds one generation to another. I can see my ancestors setting the table for Shabbat and dream about my daughters and future generations embracing this magical moment.

The meal starts roasting in the oven and the smell of Shabbat penetrates our nostrils and cuddles our souls. "Mommy, it smells Shabbat" our daughters exclaim when coming back home every Friday after school. The smell of Shabbat carves my inner self and strengthens my identity. It is about family past, present, and future.

As eighteenth-century Hassidic rabbi Levi Yitzhak of Berditchev, interpreted: "At each stage of our religious development, as our sense of God's wonder deepens, we sing differently to God--every time, we sing a new song, because each day is a new day and deserves a new song." The Hassidic master, Elimelech of Lizhensk taught: "During the six days of the week, we reach toward the Divine through the work we do in the world but on Shabbat we reach toward God through prayer and song."

I wear the appropriate clothes that identify this day as The

Special One, yet recognize in my heart that just being PRESENT is the essential requirement that intensifies our Sabbatical experience. Receiving the majestic day of Shabbat that repeats every seventh day does not become a routine. Ceremonies and rituals present a basket of emotions, memories, and a sense of belonging that makes of familiarity a warmth and path of kindheartedness that crafts the soul while embracing the moment.

Philosopher Abraham Joshua Heschel called Shabbat a "sanctuary of time" and Martin Buber refers to every Shabbat table as a "small sanctuary," reminding us of the Temple in Jerusalem. Our connection with God's creation and sense of partnership intensifies as we bring light and balminess to our homes. Shabbat is the sanctification of time, an invitation to the pinnacle in the expression of holiness.

Not this time. This Shabbat I am heading to a different experience. It will not be at my home or my synagogue. I will attend a silent retreat at the Monastery of the Holy Spirit in Conyers, Georgia. Their brochure reads:

Although the retreat experience will vary with each individual,
you can anticipate:
. The leisure to slow down, relax, and dwell with God in love.
. The opportunity to soak in a spiritual book, especially the Scriptures.
. Solitude to meditate, pray and reflect on the issues of your life.
. The worship of God, shared with monks.
. Silence to listen to the Holy Spirit bringing enlightenment and peace.
. The blessings of a deeper conversion,
purification and spiritual growth.
These and other experiences can be yours
according to God's gifts of grace.
Above all, your time at the retreat is to help you experience the
boundless love of God for YOU.
The benefits of the retreat can be summed up in

one word: PEACE-God's peace, which surpasses all
understanding. Peace that empowers you to bear God's
truth into the world, and so to BE real love for all.

To say that some of this terminology generated anxiety for me would be an understatement. Holy Spirit? Deeper conversion? Is there any agenda behind the scenes that can shake my own identity? After all, I am a Jew with a strong identity. I am a Rabbi who crossed many boundaries and taboos, opened closed doors, and overcame overwhelming rejections to become a Rabbi. I was ordained as the first female rabbi in Latin America, and completed my studies in Jerusalem exactly 20 years to the day I entered this **sacred** and **scary** place. What is a woman Rabbi doing in the Monastery of the Holy Spirit?!

Sacred and *scared* play with the same letters. Before us, the password of life develops as a mantle of choices. Is it sacred? Am I scared? **Is it both?**

This is a silent retreat. I am accustomed to speaking up. A silent retreat is an awkward place to be for a personality like mine, especially on Shabbat. On Shabbat I lead services, deliver sermons, read Torah and comment on the portion that we read that week. Shabbat is a weekly reunion with ourselves, with God, and with our family and friends. Socializing with the *Kahal*, my community, enhances Shabbat's sacred spirit week after week.

Instead of feeling lost, however, I commit myself to explore. Where would I find the voice of God which I praise every Friday evening?

The Voice of God: *Kol Adonai*. Psalm 29.

The mystic Isaac Luria (1534-1572) from the northern Israeli city of Safed pointed out that we should begin the Friday night service by reciting this psalm: The Voice of God—*Kol* Adonai. The words *kol Adonai* are repeated seven times in Psalm 29. The seven repetitions remind us of the seven days of creation, the seven rounds that we envelop in the phylacteries, the seventy times of the siege and conquest of Joshua surrounding Jericho, the seven circles around one's spouse before entering the pact of marriage, the seven steps of the *mikvah* (Jewish ritual bath), the seven stops that we do before a burial, the seven rounds of Torah (*Hakafot*) when we finish its reading and start again, the seven days of cleaning and purification before entering again into the sacredness of intimacy and sexuality, and the seven stages and levels between earth and heavens. Seven is about cycles, about renewing ourselves, about preparations to a higher purpose, and about conquering a supreme level. Seven allows us to grow in our spiritual life and emotional balance.

The welcoming of the queen—bride—*shechina*—God's feminine facet, every seventh day, deserves the majestic expression of God's voice. What happens on those days when we feel God is dysphonic? After a long week of cries, even God could lose the voice. Psalm 29 is a reaffirmation that God's voice is manifested in our cosmic life.

Rabbi Aubrey Glazer adapted the words of Yaakov Koppel Lipschitz of Mezritch (d. 1769) on Psalm 29. This is how he evoked God's manifestations:

> *At times, we hear the voice of God as thunderous and shattering as at Sinai. At other times, we hear the speaking of silence. As Elijah, the prophet, did when her returned to Sinai. The mystics ascribed specific emotions and feelings to the voices we may hear in accord with the emanations of the Divine:*
>
> *The voice of God open the gates of compassion and love.*
>
> *The voice of God opens the gates of courage*
>
> *The voice of God opens the gates of shining truth*

The voice of God opens the gates of endurance and patience

The voice of God opens the gates of splendorous beauty

The voice of God opens the gates of deepen connection

The voice of God opens the gates of presence.

The Psalm summons us to listen and hear.

I understood the concept of God's guidance in the desert with a cloud during the day and a pillar of fire at night. The desert presents a tapestry of majesty. It is an inviting place for the soul that is searching, but it also could be a dangerous one if we do not respect its nature. The desert. Desolation? Introspection? Very hot from dawn to dusk, and very cold from dusk to dawn.

While at the monastery, I took a silent walk on Shabbat (Saturday) afternoon, in the middle of the sunny heat of the Georgia summer. After many miles, I discovered a gorgeous trail where multicolor birds and elegant deer crossed my path and hid in the forest. I asked God for protection: exhausted as I was, I needed shade. Too much sun, could you please, God, cover me with clouds? The open area nearby was shaded. I looked up and thanked God.

As Shabbat enters we recite a prayer called *"Ana, B'khoach"*- literally translated as "Please, in Your Strength." The mystics ascribed the authorship of this prayer to Nechuniah ben HaKanah, who lived in the second century in the Land of Israel.

> *If You would, may your mighty right hand*
> *Undo the knot that ties us up.*
> *Accept the prayer of Your people*
> *You who are revered, raise us up, cleanse us.*
> *Almighty if You would, guard as the apple of Your eye*
> *Those who seek Your unity.*

Bless them, cleanse them, have compassion on them
Always act justly toward them.
Mighty, Holy One, in Your abundant goodness,
Guide Your people.
Alone, exalted, turn to Your people who invoke Your holiness.
Listen to our pleas, hear our cries,
Knowing the hidden depths within us.

The Shabbat experience that renews our strength every seventh day releases the knots of our constricted physical body and spiritual soul. Shabbat liberates us from enslaving habits and emancipates our constrictions tied into the material world and the cacophonic noise of the everyday life.

Rabbi Pinchas Peli (1930-1989) explained that the Jewish tradition speaks of a very interesting phenomenon concerning Shabbat: "During the week, everyone has a *neshama*, a soul. But on Shabbat we receive a *neshama y'eteira*, an extra soul. This suggests that there is some kind of undeveloped facet of personality, a spiritual dimension, of which we remain unaware. In the normal course of events, that extra soul enriches our Sabbatical experience and crafts the day with spiritual embellishment. On Shabbat, we are given the time to enrich ourselves by developing or creating this extra spiritual dimension." (Siddur Lev Shalem, The Rabbinical Assembly, page 46).

In preparation for this seventh day we praise nature and time. They sprinkle us with a refreshed spirit. And thus, says the song:

Shabbat, our Queen

The sun on the treetops no longer is seen,
Come out to welcome Shabbat, our Queen
Now she descends, the holy, the blessed
And with her, the angels of peace and of the rest.
Come, oh come, dearest bride.

Peace be unto you, you angels of peace.
With song-filled prayer we bade Shabbat welcome
And with joy in our hearts we head back home,
there the table is set, the candles burn bright,
every corner of the house glows in their light.
May you be blessed with Shabbat Shalom;
May you be blessed with Shabbat Shalom
Shalom to you, angels of peace.

(Shabbat HaMalkah by
Chaim Nahman Bialik, 1873-1934)

Accustomed to the spirit of Shabbat where we create a safe haven of spiritual sanity week after week, I was suddenly exposed to the unacquainted setting of the monastery. What to expect? Little did I know I would attend prayer services five times a day: 4 AM, 7 AM, 12:15 PM, 5:20 PM and 7:30 PM. While church attendance was not mandatory, I found there was a spiritual attraction that magnetized my desire to be present. My constant thirst for learning awoke my curiosity and, in this beautiful place, I found that the light of simplicity illuminated the building. The monks' undisturbed chanting enhanced the experience.

Soon I realized that the strong self confidence that accompanied me most of my life was challenged by the unpredictable. This time I was the outsider, the stranger, the ignorant, lost in many books of songs and psalms, old testament and new testament. This time I felt that the pagination of the books would not help me to follow along because I was "the other" in their midst. At the same time, I felt attracted to the essence of the moment, that particular moment of being present, of being with my **solitude self**, of BEING.

Bypassing the ritual, I was at another spiritual home, ready to explore. The monastery was a welcoming place where the essence of the Divine was palpable in the natural beauty of the region and the minimal furniture and decoration. This escape from a materialistic world into a spiritual universe with its powerful sound of silence offered an invitation to feel that, for this period of time, I do belong here. I was ready to carry new lenses and focus on the ability to discover the unaccustomed.

Intimidating? Sure, this experience was intimidating, but I did have two choices: either be paralyzed at the exposure to the unknown, or allow myself to gain strength from the new opportunities and horizons.

A graceful lady welcomed me to the monastery and explained some details and technicalities of the place. Private rooms were modest spaces filled with rich energy. Open areas allowed visitors to incorporate God's creation, and the many welcoming benches nourished the need to relax, take a deep breath, and reflect on the flexible fluidity of thoughts that come and go. A sign at reception greeted me: "All too often we speak simply to fill the space with sound, because we feel so uncomfortable with silence. But this silence is golden. Only in silence can you hear God speak to you. Only in silence can a real prayer, a heart prayer, be born. Next time you start chattering, stop and feel the silence, feel its shape, its texture, and the slowly and silently, say only what really has to be said." I start writing this chapter while I have no voice.

I have not been censured, at least not this time. My ENT doctor silenced me when polyps were discovered on my vocal cords and hemorrhagic strains were showing on the left side. I had no alternative but to rest my voice; silence would be one of the most effective therapies. Probably these polyps are a consequence of "abusing" my vocal cords and the damage could be permanent if I do not take care of them.

It is hard not to have a voice. It is hard not to speak up while many thoughts overwhelm your being and assault your thoughts. Voice, mouth, and tongue are the tools we use to express ourselves, to convey our essence, and to carve the imprint in the fundamental nature of our lives. We own our thoughts and we are slaves of our words. This is why we should choose our words carefully. The power of our words can build and destroy. It depends on the way we use them. How constructive or destructive is the articulation of our lexicon.

Words are powerful, but silence is too. There is power in silence, a tremendous piercing power of self-encounter and deep connection with the inner self. In the Talmud, silence is described as wisdom. The Rabbis allude to it as a "fence that protects the Torah.". In the cacophonic world that awakens our senses it is hard to find silence. That harsh, discordant mixture of sounds confuses our minds and detaches us from peace. How do we unplug ourselves from the connectivity that wires our minds, bodies and souls in a constant demanding act of being?

Rabbis of the Talmud valued silence as a vital factor of survival. Rabban Gamliel stated: "All of my life I was privileged to be in the company of wise men of Torah and I have learned from them that nothing is more valuable to productive living than silence." Silence articulates our ability to take control on logorrhea-- discourse that confuses and noises our internal self with excessive trivial talkativeness.

Silence is pregnant with the opportunities of reflections, reconnection, and returns. Religions inspire our sacred silence. The word religion comes from the Latin word *religare* and imbues its etiology to the intimate concept of binding and connecting with God. Silence, praise, songs, sounds, and stillness are routes of connection and bonds.

Let us take, for example, the notes of sheet music-- the handwritten or printed form of music notation that translates into melodies. It is the silence between those notes, the pause, that transforms noise into a delightful composition. Silence makes music. Those melodies trapped in the confusing scales and lengths of notes and cleaves become a symphony for our souls when are separated by silence. Without silence, there is no music.

Silence is needed for the articulation of our words. The breathing between words and sentences allow us to express ourselves. Silence is the space between dissonances of words. Words need silence to articulate meaning.

I found myself in the midst of a new narrative, the profound experience of silence.

My thoughts come and go in a chaotic highway full of traffic. I can visualize the synaptic connection of dendrites and axons, the feeling of channels and neurotransmitters that surpass any imagination: one, two, millions, billions, trillions of connections that conduct each thought.

Silence is an invitation to reflect on the reflection and refraction of the self. It is pregnant with messages that are yet to be discovered, the hidden presence of the occult manifesting through a potent awareness of the endless possibilities. Silence is not the absence of sounds; it is the absence of noise. **There is a plentiful presence of sounds in the flow of silence that claims from the depths its existence.** Silence may disguise loneliness and solitude, or it can open the endless possibilities of an encounter with God, self, a fellow human, the world. Silence is an invitation to contemplate.

Silence allows out to dive in the deep ocean of vast presence. Silence is not absence; it is presence. The stillness of time and space is enveloped in the pause from noises and sounds. The magic of contemplation is invited through silence and that feeling is manifested with an aura of muteness.

This book is designed to become a source of Expressions and Impressions. It is an invitation to awareness, a path to balance, and a basin that journeys. I hope it takes you from the uncomfortable and unknown to a rediscovery of the comforts of new adventures. I hope you it helps you to transform from scariness into sacredness.

The Expressions will utter your voice, pronouncing, declaring and articulating your thoughts.

The Impressions is the path to the inner self, the comfortable and warmth of snuggling with the self.

There are manifestations of silence and voices in both expressions and impressions. I invite you to journey both paths.

1.To everything there is a season, and a time to every purpose under the heaven:

2A time to be born, and a time to die; a time to plant, and a time to pluck up that which is planted;

A time to kill, and a time to heal; a time to break down, and a time to build up;

4A time to weep, and a time to laugh; a time to mourn, and a time to dance;

5A time to cast away stones, and a time to gather stones together; a time to embrace, and a time to refrain from embracing;

6A time to get, and a time to lose; a time to keep, and a time to cast away;

*7A time to rend, and a time to sew; **a time to keep silence, and a time to speak;***

Ecclesiastes 3:1-7. KJV

Silence.

To Zack.

By Analia Bortz.

Tumultuous serenity
Convoluted peace
Still lay down those bury dreams
Of potential, crippled by the shallow waters
And the sharp rocks that stole your walk.
Like a fantasy that evaporates
Through the twilight of ambiguity
Rebirth from darkness
Light from dusk
The silent prayer of recovery
The salty tears of desperation
The concealed acceptance of destiny
The cry. The Shout.
Resilience.
Birth.
When everything seems death
And later proves to be alive.
The cry. The shout.
Of a child, a new link
A new life.
A new reason to become.

YOUR PERSONAL CONTEMPLATION

Two

EXPOSURE TO FRAGILITY

So, teach *us* to number our days, that we may apply *our* hearts unto wisdom"

(Psalm 90:12, KJV)

The psalmist engages to explore the meaning of each day, helping us to experience the reality and transform it from ordinary into extraordinary. The routine of our days could be a tedious enterprise if we absorb it as a concatenated group of events and episodes that repeat every twenty-four hours. What if, instead of that uninteresting reiteration, we approach our daily reality into a majestic tray of opportunities?

We read in our liturgy *"HaMechadesh bechol yom tamid ma'aseh Breshit"* **the One Who Renews Every Day the Experience of Creation**. This is God recreating that experience, making it interesting and unique, every day. We are God's partners in the recreation of God's creation and, every morning, that chance is presented again in front of us. The light looks dimmed on some of those days and the prospects of opportunities might have shattered in front of us. Alternatives are served to confront those melancholic days. The universe looks shattered. How do we act?

Through mysticism, more precisely the theosophical kabbalah, we can **mentor** our journey by penetrating the lenses of cosmic development in our relationship with God and the universe. This is how the Kabbalistic approach would explain the cycle:

Tzimtzum-Shevirat HaKelim-Tikkun

One of the many interpretations of Kabbalah-- Jewish Mysticism, opens a world of understanding, exploring the spectrum of God's creation in partnership with humankind. The mystical tradition in its Lurianic aspect (Isaac Luria 1534-1572) voices the process of *Tzimtzum* (Contraction), Shevirat HaKelim (Broken Vessels) and Tikkun (Repair).

Tzimtzum: Contraction

Contraction is the ability to retrench. Retrenching is reducing and limiting ourselves; it is about the sense of narrowness, constriction and restriction. God does contract, either by God's upsetting relationship with God's creation in certain periods of historic time or by allowing the universe to function without micromanaging every aspect of the universe.

Tzimtzum is also a chance to give space, to ourselves and our inner beings. The contraction and constriction that drowns us into the abyss of an anoxic desperation restarts as a vast field of void filled with endless potentiality. The aptitude of breathing allows the air that expands in our alveoli to enter and leave. Any of the many tiny air sacs of the lungs which allow for rapid gaseous exchange, expands and contracts...gives space and fosters it. Each gaseous exchange cleans the toxic stage of stagnation. Expand- Retract. Play the game of being alive and live it. Contract- Relax. Find the space in between.

Shevirat HaKelim: Broken vessels.

God's emanations and attributions are contained in metaphorical vessels. These vessels have channels that communicate with each other to create a harmonious turgid balance among God's characteristics, such as judgment and compassion, strength and grandeur. The consequence of God's *tzimtzum* (contraction) creates *shevirat hakelim* (broken vessels). The consequence of OUR personal contraction, creates OUR broken vessels.

Have you ever felt a metaphorical ocean filled with broken pieces' floating in front of you, shaping horizons and wounding a scheme of unfulfilled dreams?

Those broken vessels might restrict the access to completeness, might limit the prospect of wholeness. On the other hand, broken vessels are fragments that build a mosaic, a new piece of art. The vessels contain God's emanations, those attributes that allow us to capture God's essences. We strive to reach out to those qualities throughout our lives, to improve our being and emulate God, as partners in this Divine creation. Although God's powers have shattered as a consequence of *Tzimtzum* and the contraction is displayed in God's retirement from the immanent presence, these broken vessels expand the *nitzotzot,* the **sparks**, that inspire us to repair this world through the practice of *tikkun olam,* performing deeds of living kindness. What's our responsibility? To recompose those broken vessels and recreate harmony. How do we achieve this monumental goal? By taking action, through the process of *Tikkun Olam* (repairing the world).

Tikkun: Repair

The earliest reference to *Tikkun Olam* is in the *Mishnah,* a codifying series of tractate that explain the Torah and the way of living according to the Jewish law and tradition (circa 200 CE).[1] In the daily prayer of *Aleinu,* at the conclusion of each worshiping service, the second paragraph states "we therefore place our hope on You, that we might see the glorious power...perfecting the world by Your sovereignty." We, as a reflection of God's creation, are inspired to perfect this world-- repairing it through good deeds.

In 1964, Rabbi Abraham Isaac Kook, Chief Rabbi of Israel, suggested that *Tikkun Olam* is much more than an introspective attitude of self-reparation (as proposed by Luria in the sixteenth century). Rather, *tikkun olam* requires commitment, involvement, and action for the betterment of this world. Small and large acts of loving kindness are the necessary steps to bring reparation to a world that cries for justice and peace.

Our acts in the world live to the potential of transformation. Refraction and reflection of the light that we might bring into this world are the necessary instruments for change. Our acts reflect a light that surpasses the boundaries of understanding.

---

[1] In the *Mishna Gittin* 4:2, *Tikkun Olam* refers to "promoting general welfare".

YOUR PERSONAL CONTEMPLATION

BIBLICAL AND
LITURGICAL MOMENTS
OF SILENCE

"Don't talk unless you can improve the silence."

--Jorge Luis Borges.

Silence and Voice in Biblical Characters

Characters in the Hebrew Bible suggest a cacophonic range of emotions. The strident clamor transpires in the dysfunctionality of families and relationships and illustrates the humanity of a text to which we can relate. The characters and the roles they play in a systemic paradigm are not perfect-- just the opposite. In their imperfection, we find them. They are approachable. Sometimes they reflect a familiar personality with whom we might identify.

Adam-Eve- Snake. A trilogy.

In the beginning, only God spoke. The first two chapters of the Hebrew Bible are a display of God's *creatio ex nihilo*, creation from nothing: merely God's power is involved. The angels are viewed as the "advisory board of directors" but keep quiet, without manifesting any opinion. Adam accepts the final product of his future companion:

> "And Adam said, this *is* now bone of my bones, and flesh of my flesh: she shall be called Woman, because she was taken out of Man.
>
> *(Genesis 2:23, KJV)*

and Eve is created. Now, we are two. Now, we start building up in pairs. Now, dialogue starts. Now, the ups and the downs of a relationship bond and weave into the development of an association.

Ayekah? Where are you? Genesis 3:8

The first dialogue between God and humanity is aborted in a question answered with a shameful hidden attitude. Adam hides from God, because his nakedness and full disclosure violated the integrity of the Divine-Human relationship.

We can hear the echo of God's voice that reverberates in the Garden of Eden, that wide-ranging expression that Arthur Green calls "the essential question to which our conscious must reply." Does God need a GPS device to follow Adam's pathway?

It is there, in the mystery of the unknown facing the vulnerability of life, that we find our own nakedness. Where are we? Where is the self? What are we hiding from? Ambulating in our own gardens we find trees of joy and sorrow, confidence and adversities; trees of opportunities and obstacles; trees of acceptance and rejections; trees filled with light and others filled with darkness.

Ayekah can be read as *Eicha,* **how are you?** Same exact Hebrew letters, same exact order. The intense-loud-penetrating-self provocative questions of **how** and **where** are we. Are we ready to answer with confrontational discourses? Adam was afraid; immediately he hid. Are we going to act as Adam did, with an evasive reaction, transferring the culpability to Eve? Are we going to take responsibility for our own actions?

And the LORD God called unto Adam, and said unto him, Where *art* thou? ¹⁰And he said, I heard thy voice in the garden, and I *was* naked; and I hid myself. ¹¹And he said, Who told thee that thou *wast* naked? Hast thou eaten of the tree, whereof I commanded thee that thou shouldest not eat? ¹²And the man said, **The woman whom thou gavest *to be* with me, she gave me of the tree, and I did eat.**

(Genesis 3:9-12, KVJ)

Rabbi Abraham Isaac Kook welcomes us into an illuminated forest. He expresses it under the umbrella of what we strive for:

> *"The realm of mystery tells us; you live in a world full of light and life. Know the great reality, the richness of existence that you always encounter. Contemplate its grandeur, its beauty, its precision and its harmony. The perception that dawns on a person to see the world not as finished, but as in the process of continued becoming, ascending, developing, changes that person from being "under the sun" to being "above the sun", from the place where there is nothing new to the place where there is nothing old, where everything takes on new form. The joy of heaven and earth abides on the human being as on the day of creation. In every corner where you turn, you are dealing with realities that have life, you always perform consequential acts,*

abounding with meaning and with the preciousness of vibrant life. In everything you do, you encounter sparks full of life and light, aspiring to raise towards the heights. You help those sparks and they help you."

(translated by Rabbi Ben Zion Bokser)

This forest is an open field of space and time to hide and disclose, to remain silent or engage in dialogue, to be ashamed or cultivate the self. Let us look at the garden of Eden through the lenses of opportunity. The hidden secrets of slumbered sparks.

The snake is a manifestation of evolvement. Becoming the icon of health disciplines, the snake seems witty, awake, and sheds its skin to pretend to be immortal. This reptile opens the gates for dialogue and inquiry search. Can we try something different from what God suggests?

The snake may be viewed as the source of temptation and deviation, but it is silenced and punished. It must crawl for the rest of its history. Maybe the crawling is not a punishment? Maybe it is an indication of looking closer to what is happening on earth? Its pace is precise and contemplative. Slow down, there is danger; hurry up, there is opportunity. The snake invites us to take risks and be responsible for the consequences of taking those risks. It invites us to try and to regret not having tried. We could shed the skin of fears and paralysis confronting the unknown and grow a new skin of chances and choices.

Eve, the first woman who inhabits the Garden, may be viewed as courageous rather than disobedient. Eve wants to explore, to seek. Eve wants to experience life beyond animalistic understandings; and so, when she takes that bite that opens her eyes, her gift to her descendants becomes life. Eve saves us from the tedious monotony of waking up every day in the Garden of Eden, where everything will be served on a silver platter. Eve challenges our being by exploring the endless opportunities that life presents us. Now, we are responsible for our actions; our free will is at stake and we need to own our success and failures.

The Talmudic text relates, in the context of Eve's standing as the mother of all living, that one of the known idols was in the form of a woman nursing an infant. This figure symbolized Eve, who nursed the entire world (BT *Avodah Zarah* 43a). Eve, Havvah, the mother of all life, brings life alive.

Abraham

Abraham speaks up to claim justice for the righteous people of Sodom and Gomorrah and keeps silent when God asks him to sacrifice his own, precious child. The angel calls him twice to stop the action of his hand and avoid the sacrifice of Isaac and, passively, Abraham obeys. Physically there is no sacrifice; emotionally the relationship is broken. What would have happened if Abraham's neurological connections would have prevented him from stopping that action? **Would he have been able to control the impulse that counteracts against the natural nurturing devotion of a filial relationship?** Was that voice of *"Lech Lecha"*- "Go for yourself" guided by God to an uncertain promise, stronger than the instinct of preservation? **What if the involuntary reaction that mirrors a reflex of blind faith would have occurred?** The obedience to God's request, led by blind faith, could end up in the atrocity of human sacrifice. Is that what God intended? Who is testing whom? Is it God testing Abraham to see how far a human being—a product of God's creation-- will go to obey as a knight of faith? Is it Abraham testing God by acting with uncontrollable and radical devotion? Telling God, "See, it is dangerous to request the unnatural, the unthinkable. Humans can stretch to endless possibilities and commit atrocities, just ask them."

Abraham speaks up to claim justice for the righteous people of Sodom and Gomorrah and keeps silent when God asks him to sacrifice his own son. The angel calls him twice to stop the action of his hand and avoid the sacrifice and **eagerly** Abraham obeys. Abraham is intoxicated in frantic way to obey, blindly, God's request. Abraham's radicalization raises the concern of fanaticism, extremist acting in the name of God. **Who is testing whom?**

God put Abraham to the test according to the text, but is it true?

The hidden dialogue of a manipulative relationship in which the veiled understanding of power encounters its challenge through concealed dialogue morphs into the game of dominance. Abraham, Av Ram, the father on high, the elevated, prominent and superior who stands up for the "other's" rights and claims for justice.

> *Av Ram, Abraham who challenges God asking "Peradventure there be fifty righteous within the city: wilt thou also destroy and not spare the place for the fifty righteous that are therein?*
>
> ***25**That be far from thee to do after this manner, to slay the righteous with the wicked: and that the righteous should be as the wicked, that be far from thee: Shall not the Judge of all the earth do right?*
>
> ***26**And the LORD said, If I find in Sodom fifty righteous within the city, then I will spare all the place for their sakes.*
>
> *... (Genesis 18:24-26, KJV)*

"Abraham", and he answered, *Hineni*, 'Here I am'. Abraham's attitude is to respond with certainty, to implement his entire presence, and to be present. Abraham does not hide as Adam did in the Garden of Eden. When Adam was asked "Ayekah-Where are you?" the audience would have expected an answer to that first verbal interaction between God and humanity to be "Hineni-Here I am." Instead, the text illustrates Adam's shame when it reflects his attitude in hiding and refracts his reaction on blaming the other (Eve) for his temptation. Adam doesn't take responsibility. Abraham reveals his entire SELF.

> And God said 'And it came to pass after these things, that God did tempt Abraham, and said unto him, Abraham: and he said, Behold, *here* I *am*.
>
> **2**And he said, Take now thy son, thine only *son* Isaac, whom thou lovest, and get thee into the land of Moriah; and offer him there for a burnt offering upon one of the mountains which I will tell thee of.
>
> **3**And Abraham rose up early in the morning, and saddled his ass, and took two of his young men with him, and Isaac his son, and clave the wood for the burnt offering, and rose up, and went unto the place of which God had told him.
>
> (Genesis 22:1-3. KJV)

Rabbi Gunter Plaut first quoted the nineteenth-twentieth century German philosopher Franz Rosenzweig's understanding of the whole idea of God tempting man. God must, at times, conceal his true purpose. He must mislead man (as he misled Abraham into thinking that he was the kind of God who demanded that a murder be committed for his glorification) because if were clear men would become automatons. In Rosenzweig's words, 'the most unfree, the timid and the fearful would be the most pious. But evidently God wants only the free to be His: He must make it difficult, yet impossible, to understand His actions, so as to give man the opportunity to believe, that is, to ground his faith in trust and freedom. Plaut continued: 'What kind of God is He? How can the compassionate God of the Bible, be presented as asking the sacrifice of a child?'

Plaut replied by referring to two different solutions that have been offered. The first is that the test came out of a time when human sacrifice was still an acceptable possibility; in terms of its own age, therefore, it was merely the extreme test and, after all, God did not exact the final price. The real test of faith and obedience consists in being ready to do the totally unexpected, the impossible, for the sake of God.

The other solution is that God never intended the sacrifice to be made. According to this way of reading the narrative, Abraham's test both succeeded and failed. Like the prophet who chastises his people and warns them to repent, the task is bordering on the impossible. If people repent, the prophecy of destruction fails. If people do not repent, destruction and void takes over. The prophecy prevails but the consequences are devastating. The conundrum of the prophet's task alters the course of right and wrong. Abraham's test succeeded in that it proved Abraham to be a man of faith and obedience, and it failed in that Abraham's understanding of God's nature remained deficient.

We are mesmerized by Abraham's silence. The iconic figure of Abraham, the knight of faith according to Soren Kierkegaard's description, remains silent in the most crucial moment of his life. Abraham is a wealthy man, blessed by God with many material possessions. He reaches his goal of having heirs and descendants; now exposed to the vulnerability of life, he remains silent. What paralyzes his voice and frees his body to action? Is it a dissociation of his emotional reaction from the sacrifice that faith demands from him? He wakes up EARLY in the morning, without questioning, and saddles his own animal. He does it himself instead of waiting for his servants to perform this task, and without questioning, he remains silent.

Kierkegaard's attitude can imagine God commanding

Abraham to slay his son. True the order is revoked at the last moment but the point has been made nonetheless. In Kierkegaard's terminology, there can be, so far as 'the knight of faith' is concerned, a 'teleological suspension of the ethical.' As 'ethical man' as well as 'knight of faith,' Abraham goes in 'fear and trembling' but the ultimate for him is not the ethical norm, but his individual relationship to his God.

How could God have ordered a man to murder his son? The problem is aggravated by the fact that several times in the Bible child sacrifice is condemned as an abomination before God. Arising out of the initial problem are the further questions regarding Abraham's intention to carry out the terrible deed.

> And thou shalt not let any of thy seed pass through *the fire* to Molech, neither shalt thou profane the name of thy God: I *am* the LORD.
>
> (Leviticus 18:21, KJV)

"And the LORD spoke unto Moses, saying,

> **2**Again, thou shalt say to the children of Israel, Whosoever *he be* of the children of Israel, or of the strangers that sojourn in Israel, that giveth *any* of his seed unto Molech; he shall surely be put to death: the people of the land shall stone him with stones.
>
> **3**And I will set my face against that man, and will cut him off from among his people; because he hath given of his seed unto Molech, to defile my sanctuary, and to profane my holy name.
>
> Leviticus 20:1-3,KJV

Thou shalt not do so unto the LORD thy God: for every abomination to the LORD, which he hateth, have they done unto their gods; for even their sons and their daughters they have burnt in the fire to their gods.

(Deuteronomy 12:31, KJV)

But he walked in the way of the kings of Israel, yea, and made his son to pass through the fire, according to the abominations of the heathen, whom the LORD cast out from before the children of Israel.

Kings II 16:3, KJV

And they have built the high places of Tophet, which *is* in the valley of the son of Hinnom, to burn their sons and their daughters in the fire; which I commanded *them* not, neither came it into my heart.

Jeremiah 7:31, KJV

For when ye offer your gifts, when ye make your sons to pass through the fire, ye pollute yourselves with all your idols, even unto this day: and shall I be enquired of by you, O house of Israel? *As* I live, saith the Lord GOD, I will not be enquired of by you.

Ezekiel 20:31, KJV

Will the LORD be pleased with thousands of rams, *or* with ten thousand of rivers of oil? shall I give my firstborn *for* my transgression, the fruit of my body *for* the sin of my soul?

8He hath shewed thee, O man, what *is* good; and what doth the LORD requires of thee, but to do

justly, and to love mercy, and to walk humbly with
thy God?

Micah 6: 7-8, KJV

Moreover, he burnt incense in the valley of the son
of Hinnom, and burnt his children in the fire, after
the abominations of the heathen whom the LORD
had cast out before the children of Israel.

Chronicles II 28:3

As Soren Kierkegaard articulates in <u>Fear and Trembling</u>,
published in 1843 under the pseudonym "John of the Silence,"
Abraham is culpable for the attempted murder of his son.

> *When one person sees one thing and another sees
> something else in the same thing, then the one discovers
> what the other conceals. Insofar as the object viewed
> belongs to the external world, then how the observer
> is constituted is probably less important, or, more
> correctly then what is necessary for the observation
> is something irrelevant to his deeper nature. But the
> more the object of observation belongs to the world of
> the spirit, the more important is the way he himself is
> constituted in his innermost nature, because everything
> spiritual is appropriated only in freedom; but what
> is appropriated in freedom is also brought forth. The
> difference, then, is not the external but the internal,
> and everything that makes a person impure and his
> observation impure comes from within.*

Søren Kierkegaard,
Three Upbuilding Discourses,
1843, Hong p. 59-60

The Torah speaks about the "circumcision of our hearts" when commanded to take care of those in need such as the widow, orphan, stranger and poor. Is Abraham unable to circumcise his rationality and face God's request with an inquisitive attitude?

Where is Sarah? Whispers the inner voice...

Where is Sarah? Cries the inner voice...

Where is Sarah? Shouts the inner voice with desperate wailing. Is she sleeping? Is she captive of her own disbelief? Sarah is a prey of slumber in this chapter whose author erases her cry. Why is she unseen at this critical chiasmic moment? Is Sarah recounting the days when she, herself, sacrificed Hagar and Ishmael. Is she ignored and therefore silenced? Abraham and Isaac returned from Mount Moriah where the binding took place and **where the unbinding developed an eternal silence**. There is no more dialogue between Abraham and Isaac in the rest of the biblical text. The muteness indicates the broken bond of the bind-unbind.

A cataract of the emotions unspoken says it all.

Silence prevails opening the ocean of interpretations.

There is so much dialogue in silence.

An Ode to Intoxication: Abraham

By Analia Bortz

Should I bless you, dear child?

Confused in the sopor of duty

You left behind the treasure

Of the boy, the promise

Your future.

Should I bless you, dear child?

Was that God demand from you?

To walk humbly?

To pursue justice?

To act with kindness?

To make peace?

Should I bless you, dear child?

Choosiness has confused you.

Go for yourself.

You need your silence, your inner space

To find your place.

To appease your soul.

To return, as you go.

Isaac

> "And Abraham took the wood of the burnt offering, and laid *it* upon Isaac his son; and he took the fire in his hand, and a knife; and they went both of them together.
>
> 7And Isaac spoke unto Abraham his father, and said, My father: and he said, Here *am* I, my son. And he said, Behold the fire and the wood: but where *is* the lamb for a burnt offering?
>
> 8And Abraham said, My son, God will provide himself a lamb for a burnt offering: so they went both of them **together.**
>
> Genesis 22: 6-8, KJV

This "togetherness" evaporates in the process of the "binding", the proto-pseudo sacrifice of his beloved son, Isaac. There is no physical sacrifice but the emotional murder breaks their bond forever. The text returns after this breathtaking episode showing us that Abraham returned to his servants (Genesis 22:19).

Where is Isaac? Is he bleeding from the wounds of a broken connection? Is he crying left in the abandonment? Why did *"Abba-Father"* sacrifice me? Does my mother know about it? Where are you mother? Truncated liaison that shatters the whole universe of a father-son connection. GONE.

And Isaac remains silent. He has been silenced by the shocking behavior of his father Abraham. There is no dialogue. Abraham and Isaac do not speak EVER again. The sacrifice happened. It killed the civilized words of communication. Broken relationships are the consequences of the missing words or the quiet silence.

As Kierkegaard wrote, the problem with the Biblical story of the Binding of Isaac is in its very first words: "And God said." Abraham knows that God has spoken to him, and so his faith, while tested, is still immature. Given that certainty, even sacrificing one's own son is, in a sense, reasonable. The problem of the modern faithful, however, is God's silence. We are not Abraham. We don't know if God is speaking to us or not. Perhaps it is just the bicameral mind, a voice from within that sounds like it is from without. Perhaps we are simply talking to ourselves. Thus, we must make our home in doubt, not certainty.

Where is Isaac's screaming at his father? Did he lose his voice? Indeed, he did. The text screams. The text demands attention. How do WE, today, sacrifice relationships, replacing them for ego-fed success? How do we define that success? Traumatized by what could have been, Isaac amputates the limbs of liaison that weaves their common past and barren the prospect of a solid future.

Admiel Kosman explains in his commentary <u>The Meaning of Sacrifices</u> <u>for Contemporary Believers</u> (Siddur Lev Shalem, The Rabbinical Assembly, page 188a): "Most contemporaries understand the demand for the return of sacrifice metaphorically. It may mean as William James offered, 'The sacrifice of the heart, the sacrifice of the inner ego.' Even traditionalists who believe in the efficiency of sacrifice must say that atonement for the sin and the soul's purification, the aim of sacrifice, can be achieved through the overcoming of arrogance and the diminution of the ego. As Martin Buber expressed, "Truly there is no cosmos for the human being except when the totality is made home, a temple in which one offer's one's sacrifice."

When do you hear the voice of God? Contemporary believers are caught in a conundrum. If they never hear God speaking, or even acting in ways consonant with theology, then surely they must doubt God's very existence. And yet if they do claim to hear a *bat kol* – a Divine voice – surely, they must doubt their sanity.

In Martin Scorsese's lyrical, paradoxical new depiction of faith, "Silence," the young Jesuit priest Rodriguez, played by Andrew

Garfield, pleads in desperation for God to answer him as he watches the faithful suffer. For a Jewish audience, this Catholic priest on a mission in medieval Japan is an oddly familiar figure, reminding one of religious Jews in the Holocaust, wondering how God could allow evil to triumph unchecked. It's like Job, who did not sin with his lips but probably did with his heart. Cursing God for his devastating faith, when his family and possessions are taken from him.

How to understand evil? Can we justify the concept of "Banality of Evil"? This book and the concept of banality of evil coined by Hannah Arendt, a political theorist who wrote in 1963, after witnessing the trial against the Nazi Adolph Eichmann's in Jerusalem, arrives to the conclusion that Eichmann should not be displayed as a guilty man for the actions he committed during the Nazi regime because he was simply doing his job, performing his duty, obeying the law imposed on him by the Nazi party. Hannah Arendt's conclusion, shakes my core values of right and wrong.

Is it appropriate to bring order into the chaos of the unbearable? Suffering, abandonment, gregarious apathy call for social responsibility. It is the incomprehensible feelings of evil that take over the voices that clamor for justice. As Abraham Joshua Heschel taught, "In a free society, when evil is done, some are guilty; all are responsible." The silent cry of injustice shouts strong and steady.

Silence is thus a <u>rejection of all kinds of certainty</u>. The fake-faithful fundamentalists of today are certain that God's voice is telling them to persecute Jews, Muslims, gays, women, and many others. Oppression is done in the name of God. Intolerance is justified in the name of God. When are, WE, planning to take responsibility, and stop this incoherent state of God's intoxication and act in a civilized manner of mutual respect, pursuing the gift of learning from diversity? Fanatics and radicals believe God is rooting for their football team, their army, their country, their piece of land.

Avi: My Father.

By Analia Bortz

The ropes that bind me to the altar hurt my skin,
Avinu, our father, father of all nations
Where is the lamb?
The lamb that would come to my rescue and
would cry my tears.
Talk to me Abba-father.
Do not remain silent.
Are you there?
I AM HERE, Abba.
Do not hide your face from me.
I'm your son, your "only" son,
your beloved one,
Isaac.
Long for your voice Abba. Where are you?
I am here. I am Isaac.
No more laughter, just tears.
No more voices, just silence.
The FATHER of all humanity, would not father me?
The JUDGE of all humanity, would not make justice?

Moses

Mary Jane Chaignot points out in Bible Wise that many scholars highlight the parallels between the stories of Moses and Hagar. Hagar lives a double life as wife and slave. Moses was born into a persecuted family, yet raised in Pharaoh's palace-- a slave and a prince. Both flee to the wilderness and feel threatened by the system. Both encounter God and are asked to return. Overcoming fears, they comply.

Hagar has a voice that is only heard from the cry of her son, and

Moses has difficulties speaking; maybe he stuttered. He has a "heavy tongue" according to the literal translation from the original Hebrew. God hears the cry of the enslaved people, not the ones from Moses.

Moses sermonizes the Israelites in the wilderness throughout the forty years. He even sings, both in the book of Exodus, after the crossing of the Sea of Reeds (wrongly translated as the Red Sea) and in his farewell poem, in the book of Deuteronomy. His voice is heard and his silence buffers the latent significance of his talking point--the underlined agenda.

> Now Moses kept the flock of Jethro his father in law, the priest of Midian: and he led the flock to the backside of the desert, and came to the mountain of God, *even* to Horeb.
>
> 2And the angel of the LORD appeared unto him in a flame of fire out of the midst of a bush: and he looked, and, behold, the bush burned with fire, and the bush *was* not consumed.
>
> 3And Moses said, I will now turn aside, and see this great sight, why the bush is not burnt.
>
> 4And when the LORD saw that he turned aside to see, God called unto him out of the midst of the bush, and said, Moses, Moses. And he said, Here *am* I.
>
> 5And he said, Draw not nigh hither: put off thy shoes from off thy feet, for the place whereon thou standest *is* holy ground."
>
> *Exodus 3:2-5, KJV)*

The angel sent by God waited, and saw that that Moses gazed. Moses was capable of seeing the extraordinary. The bush aflame was not consumed. In a simple bush, something unusual was happening. Moses, a responsible shepherd, preoccupied with his flock, does not focus on the herd. For a few instances, he is aware of this extraordinary phenomenon. God sees that he is ready.

That insignificant bush becomes the flame of a collective narrative that is about to start. The land, where Moses is standing, becomes holy because, and only because, the moment is sacred. The scene is confusing and overwhelming. The scene captivates Moses' attention and the future leader stops, silently, to embrace the moment.

Abraham Joshua Heschel would call this kind of sacred moments **"radical amazement."** It's all about finding AWE. Moses is mesmerized by the miraculous occurrence. Does he worry about being caught in this fire? Is he attracted by its novelty? Is it the uniqueness of the moment, a pivotal occurrence in his life, that Moses, who is old (age 80) and a stutterer, awakens to the endless possibilities that life is still providing? What kind of voice is Moses hearing? Is it his inner self? Is that the voice of God? Is it the voice of the angel? Is it a cacophonic mishmash of unintelligible sounds or noises?

The exegetical Rabbinical comment on Midrash Exodus Rabbah 3:1 suggests that Moses heard the voice of his father, Amram. Moses' fears declined, he felt at home, he was comfortable, but it also posed the jeopardy that he could confuse or identify God with his father. Regardless of the identity of the voice, Moses gazed, stopped, heard and declared himself present. He is in, recognizing the awesomeness of the moment. The majesty of the unknown. He Is PRESENT in the moment.

In the commentary on the sixth blessing of the Amidah prayer, in the paragraph for gratitude for life, the prayer book *Siddur Lev Shalem* (page 200) expresses: "The prayer talks of the miracles that accompany us every day. Our lives are made up moments that are quite very special. At which time it is easy to express gratitude... but there is also the miracle of the everyday-- which because is it common place, we often fail to recognize: the ability to use our limbs for what we desire, the warmth of the sun, the plants around us that sustain our breathing...some of the greatest blessings initially present themselves to us concealed within disappointment, uncertainty, loss, or pain; the aspect of blessing within unfolds slowly, over time- and often only in retrospect…we approach our lives with humility and faith, recognizing that with the benefit of hindsight, what seems like darkness in our lives may contain with a blessing only later to be revealed, only later become a shining light." (Prayer book Lev Shalem, Rabbinical Assembly)

What is it hidden in this "plain bush" full of potential? Come closer Moses and see. Come close enough to stay warm but not too close to burn. Find your balance, Moses. Find the way to connect without erasing your own identity. Find the distance of the self as well as come close enough to hear the cry.

Let us take a closer look at the burning bush dialogue:

> "And Moses said unto God, Who *am* I, that I should go unto Pharaoh, and that I should bring forth the children of Israel out of Egypt?"
>
> (Exodus 3:11, KJV).

MI ANOCHI "Who am I that I should go to Pharaoh?" said Moses to God. "And how can I possibly get the Israelites out of Egypt?" On the surface the meaning is clear. Moses is asking two things. The first: who am I, to be worthy of so great a mission? The second: how can I possibly succeed? Who is Moses? Does he understand the cry of suffering in Egypt? Raised as a prince and fleeing from his palace instead of confronting the reality of injustice and murder, is he the right person? Moses is surprised by God's selection. He might ask himself, isn't there anybody else, more skilled to carry that monumental endeavor of confronting Pharaoh, the most powerful man on earth? Moses is now a simple shepherd and, in its simplicity, he gets chosen?

He is not blinded by the wealth of Pharaoh's palace or deaf to the environment that surrounds him. Has Moses become more aware of his surroundings? Establishing a distance from the boisterous Egypt would give him a different perspective? Is God trying to remind him of his origin and identity when God mentions the cries in Egypt?

When Moses asks, "Who am I?" it is not just that he feels himself unworthy. He feels himself uninvolved. Did apathy take over his Israelite origin? "Your fathers' God sent to me, he will tell his brothers and sisters oppressed in Egypt. **YOUR** fathers' God. Not mine.

Rabbi Joseph Soloveitchik called this a covenant of fate, *brit goral*. A common destiny. Getting involved in a common destiny- -feel the connection with your ancestors and be responsible for your people's fortune-- is intrinsically a call that demands to be answered. Moses must figure out why was he chosen for this colossal task. **Who am I?** asked Moses; he knew the answer. Deep in his heart, Moses looks at his inner self. He is not Moses the Egyptian anymore. He is not Moses the Mydianite anymore. Now, he is the leader of a nation. He sees suffering and answers the call. God never answered the first question.

Moses' second question to God at the burning bush was, "Who are you?"

> "And Moses said unto God, Behold, *when* I come unto the children of Israel, and shall say unto them, The God of your fathers hath sent me unto you; and they shall say to me, What *is* his name? what shall I say unto them?"
>
> (Exodus. 3:13, KJV).

God's reply, ***Ehyeh asher ehyeh*** - I will be who I will be – is often wrongly translated as "I am that I am." Ehyeh-- I will be-- is the endless possibility of finding God, in past, present and future. There is no conjugation of "to be" in the present tense in Hebrew. *Ehyeh* is a permanent flowing, transcending above time and space. *Ehyeh* is the open gate to look for God.

We read in our everyday liturgy from the book of Chronicles *"Ismach Ha Lev Mebakshey Adonai."* Happy is the heart that SEEKs for God. It does not say that FINDS GOD. The emphasis is stressed in the seeker, a dynamic process who does not conform to the status quo, a self-motivator on exploring and discovering.

Take off your shoes. Moses. You just
consecrated this place as a holy one.

Rabbi Shlomo Ephraim ben Aaron of Luntchitz (1550-1619) commented on the above passage: *"Take off your shoes...The world is always full of sharp objects and stones. When one wears shoes, we can easily step on the small stones lying on the way, almost without feeling them. However, when one walks barefoot, humankind feels every small thing lying on the ground, every thorn, every painful stone. God said to Moses, the leader of Israel, "Take off your shoes". The leader of the generation must feel every obstacle and every impediment on the road. The leader must feel the pain of the people and realize what is constricting them."*

The ability to hear and feel the voices of the desperate leads to the capacity of embracing those voices and guides them towards salvation. Only when we empathize with the voices and the silence of the others, do we understand the depth of the tacit dialogue. To UNDERSTAND is to STAND UNDER, to get to the depth, to penetrate the shallowness and dive into the meaning of relationship.

Moses, who spends the last 40 years of his life teaching statutes and commandments, describes himself as *arel sefatayim*, a man of "uncircumcised lips", a man of "sealed lips".

"And Moses said before the LORD, Behold, I *am* of
uncircumcised lips, and how shall Pharaoh hearken
unto me?

(Exodus 6:30, KJV)

What does it mean to have lips with a foreskin? Does it make him unable to talk? Moses spends four out of five books of the Pentateuch talking after all! Is the message holy enough, sacred enough, pure enough to enable him to cure this potential phimosis by removing this impediment that restricts him in his comfort zone as a shepherd, and become the ongoing and unconditional leader of the Israelites? This is Moses, the one who overcomes his speech impediment and leads an arduous flock towards the unknown. Our sages address this development of Moses' attitude in the exegetical explanation *Midrash Rabbah -Deuteronomy:*

> "And Moses said unto the LORD, O my Lord,
> I *am* not eloquent, neither heretofore, nor since
> thou hast spoken unto thy servant: but I *am* slow
> of speech, and of a slow tongue.'

> (Exodus 4:10, KJV)

But once he merited the Torah, his tongue was healed, and he began to speak the words, which we recite in the matter of, 'These are the words which Moshe spoke.'

The transformative image of Moses from his speech impediment to the great leader.

All too often we speak simply to fill the space with sound, because we feel so uncomfortable with silence. But this silence is golden. Only in silence can you hear God speak to you. Only in silence can a real prayer, a wholehearted prayer, be born. Next time you start chattering, stop and feel the silence, feel its shape, its texture, and then slowly and silently, say only what must be said.

Silence could be like the fruit of the cactus. The thorns outside could make us uncomfortable and oppress the need of expression, making us bleed through hemorrhagic strains of isolation. Yet, the fruit of the cactus is sweet, indulges us to crave for rediscoveries.

Aaron

Tragedy invaded the book of Leviticus. At the end of the third portion of this book called *Shemini- On the Eighth Day,* which speaks about the laws of Kashrut--body of dietary laws-- and the joy that surrounds the ritual in the Tabernacle, Aaron and his family have just been inaugurated as priests. Aaron is becoming the first High Priest. In the midst of this jubilant occasion, Aaron's two sons die.

Who kills them? A jealous fellow? A wartime enemy? A catastrophic disease? No. Nadav and Avihu are killed by God. What's Aaron's reaction?

VaYidom Aaron, And Aaron was silent.
Leviticus 10:3. (My translation)

Nadav and Avihu have ignited a "strange fire" in the midst of the inauguration of their prestigious new role as priests. What does it mean a "strange fire"-*esh zarah?* The Rabbis have tried to explain that it refers to a ritual that was not accepted by God. The chaotic moment invites them to act without boundaries or may be with a fanatic-radical approach that God cannot tolerate. The fire descends from heaven and consumes their lives. Their passion is trapped in the flames of extremism.

"They moved too close to the existence of God"
(Leviticus 16:1, my translation).

Tragedy amid joy vacuums Aaron's life. Aaron, doesn't cry of despair. He remains SILENT. How can it be? It was at that precise moment. It should have been the climax of his life. Crowned as the High Priest and surrounded by his four children who would follow in his footsteps. This should have been Aaron's time to celebrate. Instead, it was wounded by the irreparable loss of his children. He is a father twice bereaved and he does not shout out, complain, or protest. Where is Aaron's anger? Sense of injustice?

Aaron is described in the Jewish tradition as a *"rodef shalom,"* a pursuer of peace (Ethics of the Fathers-*Pirkei Avot* 1:12). He appeases the children of Israel in the wilderness when Moses disappears. Aaron is Moses' voice in front of Pharaoh; he speaks smoothly and brings harmony. Aaron bridges people's understandings. Aaron is a man of words. The flame consumes his words, burns his soul, silences his heart.

This silence is seen in the Jewish tradition as a right and proper response. The *Midrash Leviticus Rabbah* commented on this verse: "Aaron was rewarded for his silence." Which kind of reward? What could be felt a "reward" after the death of your child? In the Talmud, we find the statement that "the world is preserved only because of those who stop themselves from speaking out in difficult moments of strife" (Babylonian Talmud. Hullin 89a). Grief needs time to be healed, and we are taught not to speak to a mourner until he or she starts the conversation. Any statement could feel irrelevant when speaking to a mourner, so the wisdom of the Jewish tradition is to give room for silence when the pain is so present. Silence is another language to express the grief and it surpasses language when the unbearable is present.

The Talmudic text, in the tractate of *Zevachim* 115b, explains: "When Aharon thus perceived that his sons were the honored ones of the Omnipresent, he was silent, and was rewarded for his silence, as it is said, And Aharon held his peace. And thus, it says of David, be silent before the Lord, and wait patiently [*hith-hollel*] for Him: though God casts down many slain [*halalim*] of thee, be silent before Him. And thus, it was said by Solomon, "[There is . . .] *a time to keep silence, and a time to speak*": sometimes a man is silent and is rewarded for his silence; at others, a man speaks and is rewarded for his speaking.

When the sacred act of the Pact of Circumcision is performed in order to "enter a child into the Covenant of Abraham" one of the blessings bestowed upon the child refers to *"Be Damayich Hayii"* –in your blood you will live-.

The Dubner Maggid (Rabbi, 1740-1804. Lithuania) explains that God will respond to each one of us in critical moments, as God did listen to the silent cry of Aaron. God had listened the strident silence of Aaron. *BeDamayich chayee* can also, be translated a different way – *damayich* does not have to mean 'your blood' but 'your silence'- *DUMAYICH*- stillness, silence. YOU WILL LIVE IN YOUR SILENCE.

Silence is Aaron's antidote to the unbearable pain. It does not erase the pain. Instead, it allows time to heal wounds. The scar, which will remain forever, stops the bleeding and Aaron does not physically die with his own children.

Daughter of Jephthah

And Jephthah vowed a vow unto the LORD, and said, If thou shalt without fail deliver the children of Ammon into mine hands,

> **31**Then it shall be, that whatsoever cometh forth of the doors of my house to meet me, when I return in peace from the children of Ammon, shall surely be the LORD'S, and I will offer it up for a burnt offering.

> **32**So Jephthah passed over unto the children of Ammon to fight against them; and the LORD delivered them into his hands.

> **33**And he smote them from Aroer, even till thou come to Minnith, *even* twenty cities, and unto the plain of the vineyards, with a very great slaughter. Thus, the children of Ammon were subdued before the children of Israel.

> **34**And Jephthah came to Mizpeh unto his house, and, behold, his daughter came out to meet him with timbrels and with dances: and she *was his* only child; beside her he had neither son nor daughter.

> **35**And it came to pass, when he saw her, that he rent his clothes, and said, Alas, my daughter! thou hast brought me very low, and thou art one of them that trouble me: for I have opened my mouth unto the LORD, and I cannot go back.

> **36**And she said unto him, My father, *if* thou hast opened thy mouth unto the LORD, do to me according to that which hath proceeded out of

thy mouth; forasmuch as the LORD hath taken vengeance for thee of thine enemies, *even* of the children of Ammon.

37And she said unto her father, Let this thing be done for me: let me alone two months, that I may go up and down upon the mountains, and bewail my virginity, I and my fellows.

38And he said, Go. And he sent her away *for* two months: and she went with her companions, and bewailed her virginity upon the mountains.

39And it came to pass at the end of two months, that she returned unto her father, who did with her *according* to his vow which he had vowed: and she knew no man. And it was a custom in Israel,

40*That* the daughters of Israel went yearly to lament the daughter of Jephthah the Gileadite four days in a year.

(Judges 11:30-40, KJV)

The daughter of Jephthah does not have a name. Her tears wiped her name away, as if the salty wet fluid exuding out of her eyes, acted as a corrosive rustic balm that wounded her heart. She will be remembered as an unfulfilled chapter that did not close. **So, there arose an Israelite custom that for four days every year the daughters of Israel would go out to lament the daughter of Jephthah the Gileadite.**

And we wait for a voice from heaven to spare the dancing daughter. But unlike with Isaac, the child of promise, we hear no voice; a ram does not appear. God is silent. The daughter's well-planned routines are replaced by the rending of garments: lamentation for the loss of lineage. Today let us rend our garments: lamentation for the loss of her name.

The daughter of Jephthah is the iconic representation of the unfulfilled dreams of every girl and woman who is a victim of physical, emotional, or moral abuse. Her life was cut short and her desires were truncated by the malicious exercise of external forces. Any victim of abuse dies internally although she or he remains physically alive. The shell of the body is emptied by the vacuum that consumes the emotional self.

Jephthah's daughter does not have a name because her persona has been erased and her soul has been consumed by cruelty. The Bible remains silent. God doesn't speak up. Her father doesn't speak up. Her friends don't speak up. She is not here. She does not exist. Whom should we condemn for not allowing her to be? She cries, and dies.

> Death and life *are* in the power of the tongue: and they that love it shall eat the fruit thereof."
>
> (Proverbs 18:21, KJV)

Daughter of Jephthah: I give you a name.

By Analia Bortz

The universal cry.
The village displaced you.
You have been forgotten.
At the shores of the river, there you wept.
For you and the many more
I will share your tears.
You have been stripped away.
Your sister was too.
In Africa and Asia, in Europe and America

As a lamb to be sacrificed
By the silence of the world
And the cruelty of humankind
You became a property
An object, disposable.
Not anymore,
You have a name. You have a sound.
You have a voice.

Kol Demamah Daka.

The Voice of a Thin Stillness.

The book of Kings I Chapter 19 verse 12, relates the story of the encounter between Elijah the prophet and God. The sounds and silence dance in an epiphany, only seeing during these special moments. It is the sound of stillness--the sound of silence.

The prophet Elijah had a profound experience of Divine silence at Mount Horeb. Elijah lived in tumultuous times. The counter power between the crown and the religious establishment were at stake. Elijah worked to re-awaken the monotheistic faith of the people, who, jumping between two branches, at times placed their faith in the religion of their fathers and at other times, in that of Phoenicians (I Kings. 18:21). At the famous contest on Mount Carmel, the prophets of Baal were slaughtered in the presence of the King. Jezebel threatened Elijah's life and he fled to Mount Horeb (I Kings. 19:5- 7), the same mountain on which, centuries before, God had appeared to Moses. Here, he had a remarkable theophany. A strong wind passed, then a fire, then an earthquake, but in none of these phenomena, was God present. At the end, Elijah perceived *kol demamah dakah* – "a still small voice," or, in an alternative translation, "a thin sound of silence." The prophet, covering his face as a gesture of respect, understood that God had finally shown

Godself (19:11- 13). It was a challenging task to find God in silence, in stillness. Hidden, in the obscure unnoticed notes of muteness.

"A thin sound of silence," or the voice of an impalpable silence. A poet might say that words hide themselves in the folds of silence and, at the same time, silence keeps within itself the folds of the word.

YOUR PERSONAL CONTEMPLATION

Four

BROKEN TABLETS

What are "the broken tablets? What are the broken tablets? They are the expression of frustration and disappointments.

Who broke them? When did they break? Moses descends Mount Sinai and sees the Jewish people dancing around the golden calf. Moses takes the two tablets he is holding in his two hands and thrusts them to ground, shattering them. The divine gift of the tablets etched by God now lays strewn on the ground.

Whatever became of the tablets smashed by Moses? The Talmud answers: The broken tablets were placed in the holy Ark along with the second, intact set; "*luchot ve'shivrey luchot munachim be'aron*"-- The tablets and the broken tablets dwell in the Ark (Babylonian Talmud Bava Batra 14b). The broken tablets were not buried, which is what we generally do with holy items no longer in use. They were placed in the most sacred place, in the *Aron Hakodesh*, the holy Ark. Eventually they sat next to the second tablets, the whole set of the Ten Commandments. Together they remained securely protected as the nation journeyed through the wilderness.

Why do the broken pieces remain precious? If they represent the Jewish people disregarding the covenant with God, would we not wish to simply forget about them? The word *Luach* in Hebrew, also means calendar. Are the broken tablets a central part of our agenda? Our calendar is filled with commitments and dreams; the broken tablets are a metaphorical reminder of our vulnerability. The calendar is a reminder of our obligations, our routine, our moments of celebrations and commemorations. Laughter and sadness alternate on the piece of paper, reminding us on daily basis that we are alive with strengths and frailties.

A testimony from Devi, a member of my Congregation:

> *"The past few years I have begun to come to terms with my own broken tablets. Namely my struggle with mental illness that will stay with me always. Just as the smashed tablets that Moses brought down from Mt Sinai resided beside the 2nd set in the Ark, my health and my illness coexist in my head and my heart. And for that I believe I am a stronger person.*
>
> *This is not to say that I am happy that I have two different sets of "tablets," but it is my reality and one I am coming to terms with. My struggle with both depression and anxiety will stay with me for my entire life; I cannot discard them. I also carry with me times of good mental health that can be compared to the whole tablets. And I think I appreciate the healthy days much more because of the existence of the "bad" ones. It is important to remember, for me and my loved ones, that my different states coexist and are inextricably intertwined. I wouldn't be me without them.*
>
> *Some days I feel as if I have misplaced one set of tablets or the other. On amazing days, I often enjoy the wonderful and warm feelings and shut out any memory of the days I could barely function. Although that sounds like a great plan, it often undermines me when my mind*

starts to wander into dark places. Why? Because then I forget that I can survive and have survived awful days, weeks, months…. I begin to despair. If I keep a little of my shattered emotions with me at all times I can enjoy the light, express my gratitude and have faith that I will make it through the struggles.

Conversely, on my lowest days, when it seems like my health (whole tablets) have been lost for good, I can see no way out. It is devastating and heartbreaking. Luckily, I have a support system, an incredible one, who will call on a search party to help me find them. Of course, I have to reach out and let people know I have misplaced them. It's hard, and sometimes embarrassing, to let others in on my journey and let them know how easy it is for me to lose my wholeness, hope or way. Luckily once whatever is missing is found, I can have gratitude and appreciation, and of course great love, for those who hold me up when I can't stand on my own two feet.

I have wrestled with the reasons behind my chemical imbalance and what I have viewed as flawed mind, trying to figure out why I struggle. I am slowly realizing that my path is to help others, in little or big ways, to not feel alone, to get help, to educate. And my new calling as an advocate does make me stand a little taller, feel a little stronger and perhaps for the first time in my life - proud of myself. And that is definitely growth that wouldn't have happened without my struggles. That is just the beginning of the positive that has come about from my depression and anxiety, although on hard days I can forget to appreciate them.

Many Jewish symbolic rituals have a brokenness to them (think breaking matzah-unleavened bread- as a ritual at the Passover Seder or shattering of the glass under the canopy at the end of a Jewish wedding) which remind us of harder times in the history of our people. Our religion teaches us that our scars are not to be forgotten or ashamed of; instead they are a symbol of our strength and survival. Having these practices in my Judaism helps to ground me and remind me I am not alone, and that others have stood on similar shaky ground.

I have met many people on my journey, some who have had major impact on my life. Some acquaintances who were on the peripheral of my life have reached out and either offered support or asked for assistance. My connections and interactions with others are more authentic and I am finding my voice. I am learning to question and voice my opinion. Of course, there are many downsides to living with mental illness, but I am starting to believe that I am a better person because of it. I did not become a writer until I started to put down my thoughts on paper, suggested by my first therapist.

My hard times have imbued in me a new level of empathy. Before my biggest depressive episode, I kind of, sort of, knew how others struggled and suffered. I can now say that I really and truly get it. One hundred percent. And although I've spent countless hours crying and asking God "Why me?" and being angry at the world, I have learned so much about myself and the world through my sometimes-painful experiences.

Rabbi Harold S. Kushner, in his book When Bad Things Happen to Good People, put it so eloquently: "Pain is the price we pay for being alive...When we understand that, our question will change from, 'Why do we have to feel pain?' to 'What do we do with our pain so that it becomes meaningful and not just pointless empty suffering?'" Reading this spoke to me. Sharing my struggle and relating to and helping other people makes my suffering feel as though it has a purpose. So, I will continue to reach out and speak out and give my friends and family permission to remind me this on days when all I can find are my broken tablets."

We move through life now with two sets of tablets. There are times of joy, and there is time of great sadness. They are encased in the same box-- in the same heart. The medieval commentator Rashi says that the two sets of tablets, the broken and the whole sets, sit touching one another. The seat of the emotions is found in the heart. Here, in this one enclosed space, emotions freely move from one place to the next. We can help mend fractured hearts when we stay sensitive to those who need our empathy and support. This is how we help bring about '*shleimut*', wholeness, to a world with so many broken shards.

Human beings confront brokenness and acknowledge vulnerability. With great strength and resilience those who are broken still find the strength to lead more fulfilling and meaningful lives. Many people have admirably found the faith and willpower from within, and with the support of those around them, go on to accomplish and create great things. They have ennobled and rebuilt their lives even after suffering the deep pain of loss. This is a testament to the valiant spirit that is endowed in the soul of man. God cradles the broken tablets side by side with the whole ones in the holiest place in our tradition. The symbol of the broken tablets serves as a poignant reminder of our sacred responsibility to be ever sensitive to those who suffer and to reach out and be understanding and embracing of those who live with 'broken tablets' in their hearts.

The broken tablets are a reminder of the shattered wholeness that might become holy. It is a trial to find wholeness in the crevices of what has been fragmented.

I have been mesmerized by the way many artists dealt with their genius endeavor by overcoming difficulties.

Ludwig Van Beethoven (1770-1827)

Thirty-two-year-old Beethoven — who, in a testament to elemental hardships of the era the absence of which we now take for granted, didn't know his own date of birth at the time and believed he was twenty-eight — wrote shortly after the completion of his Second Symphony (The Heiligenstadt Testament, October 1802):

> *Oh! ye who think or declare me to be hostile, morose, and misanthropically, how unjust you are, and how little you know the secret cause of what appears thus to you! My heart and mind were ever from childhood prone to the most tender feelings of affection, and I was always disposed to accomplish something great. But you must remember that six years ago, I was attacked by an incurable malady, aggravated by unskillful physicians, deluded from year to year, too, by the hope of relief, and at length forced to the conviction of a lasting affliction (the cure of which may go on for years, and perhaps after all prove impracticable).*
>
> *Born with a passionate and excitable temperament, keenly susceptible to the pleasures of society, I was*

yet obliged early in life to isolate myself, and to pass my existence in solitude. If I at any time resolved to surmount all this, oh! how cruelly was I again, repelled by the experience, sadder than ever, of my defective hearing! — and yet I found it impossible to say to others: Speak louder; shout! for I am deaf! Alas! how could I proclaim the deficiency of a sense which ought to have been more perfect with me than with other men, —a sense which I once possessed in the highest perfection, to an extent, indeed, that few of my profession ever enjoyed! Alas, I cannot do this! Forgive me therefore when you see me withdraw from you with whom I would so gladly mingle. My misfortune is doubly severe from causing me to be misunderstood. No longer can I enjoy recreation in social intercourse, refined conversation, or mutual outpourings of thought.

Completely isolated, I only enter society when compelled to do so. I must live like an exile. In company, I am assailed by the most painful apprehensions, from the dread of being exposed to the risk of my condition being observed... What humiliation when any one beside me heard a flute in the far distance, while I heard nothing, or when others heard a shepherd singing, and I still heard nothing! Such things brought me to the verge of desperation, and well-nigh caused me to put an end to my life. Art! art alone, deterred me. Ah! how could I possibly quit the world before bringing forth all that I felt it was my vocation to produce?

Alfred Kazin-American writer and literary critic, 1915-1998-wrote in his "Introduction to William Blake": "Beethoven could not hear the world, but he always believed in it. His struggles to sustain himself in it, on the highest level of his creative self-respect, were vehement because he could never escape the tyranny of the actual." We don't define Beethoven by his deafness but by his genius how he mastered his music and how he gifted us all with his compositions.

When we label people, we become blind to their essence. Stigmas depersonalize humanity. They lose in our sight the PERSONA, and their presence is attached to the tag they carry. Labels are barriers that distance us from the transcendental being of the other.

YOUR PERSONAL CONTEMPLATION

Five

CRAFTING AND STAGING

"You have to stage your home" indicated our real estate agent when we put the house on the market. What does it mean we should "stage" our home? This is not a theatre in which we "perform" on a stage! I had never heard that terminology before.

When real estate agents talk about staging your home, they are referring to a method of decorating that is designed to showcase the home's best assets, impress buyers and sell quickly. Basically, it means to transform your product into a desirable one, to tempt potential customers.

I prefer the genuine way-- showing who you really are. It did not go well with the real estate agent.

Why Home Staging Is Important?

I did my homework and through different websites along with the help of social media, I found out about the intricate purpose of staging. Although staging is optional, it really should not be according to the new classic school of twenty first century "staging your home Philosophy class."

When you are dealing with such a significant financial

transaction, you do not want to be lazy and settle for a lower selling price or a longer marketing period than you need. Relative to the amount of time and money involved, staging may be one of the most lucrative projects you ever undertake. Potential buyers are not just looking for a structure to inhabit – they are looking to fulfill their dreams and improve their lifestyles. Staging helps sell those dreams and creates a more emotional purchase.

Home staging is also beneficial because potential buyers do not want to see work that needs to be done upon moving into the home. For every problem they see, they will deduct its cost from their offer price. If they see too many problems, they will pass altogether.

I decided to take a class on "Staging 101" trying to find the best resources to achieve the most optimal results. Weaving sources filled with advice I created a list which I have compiled below, called: *Staging Tips for a Prompt and Good Sale.*

Clean

In the kitchen, potential buyers love to see new appliances that come with the home, but if you cannot do that, make the ones you have spotless. No one wants to see splattered spaghetti sauce. Likewise, make sure your bathroom sparkles; from the corners of the tub to the sink drain to that spot behind the toilet you don't think anyone can see. You will be very surprised what people do when they come to see your house and you are not present. Your goal should be to make everything look new.

Declutter

There are two major problems with clutter, meaning MESS. One is that it distracts buyers from your home's features. The other is that it makes the home seem like it does not have enough storage space. Put away unnecessary items. Keep in mind that buyers will be interested in your closet space, so tossing everything into the closet to hide it away may not be the best strategy.

Depersonalize

Persona is a derivative of the Latin word for a theatrical mask. According to the Swiss-German analytical psychologist Carl Jung, 1865-197, the persona is the mask or appearance one presents to the world. To depersonalize your home means to remove your presence. Erase your footprints. Detach your sense of belonging. This one is the hardest one.

Buyers need to be able to envision themselves in your home, so remove all the family photos, items with family members' names on them and refrigerator art. Also, make sure to put away all the toys and anything else that is highly indicative of the home's current inhabitants. If you have kids, do not show their cute pictures or their magnificent art projects.

Eradicate Odors

What some call odors, others call perfumes. It is a subjective matter. Smells arouse memories. Pets, kids, what you ate for dinner last night, and many other conditions can make your home smell. You are probably immune to your home's smell, so you will need to have a friend or neighbor help you out with this one. There are inexpensive tricks for ridding a home of odors and giving it an inviting aroma including baking cinnamon-coated apples, burning vanilla-scented candles, or throwing some slice-and-bake cookies in the oven. It is also a good idea to grind half a lemon in the garbage disposal to remove sink odors. Finally, do not forget to take out the trash.

Define Rooms

Make sure each room has a single, defined purpose. Also, make sure that every space within each room has a purpose, so that buyers will see how to maximize the home's square footage. If you have a finished attic, make it an office. A finished basement can become an entertainment room, and a junk room can be transformed into a guest bedroom.

Paint. Never Wallpaper.

It is unlikely that a potential buyer will like your wallpaper. Your best bet is to tear it down and paint the walls instead. Don't even think about painting over the wallpaper – it will look shabby and send red flags for the buyer about all the work he or she will have to do later. It is actually better to paint your home with warm, neutral colors that appeal to the masses and project the homey image you are trying to sell.

Flooring

The place where you step your chapters of life must be immaculate, as if your pass-through life has never existed. No one wants to live with dirty, stained carpet, especially when someone else made it that way. Though pricey, hardwood floors add value and elegance to a home. They are also low-maintenance, provide great long-term value and are perfect for buyers with allergies. In other words, they appeal to almost everyone, and if not, they are easily carpeted over by the buyer and preserved for the next owner. One caveat: In kitchens and bathrooms, go with ceramic tile or stone if you can afford it.

Lighting

Do not hide yourself behind darkness. Take advantage of your home's natural light. Open all curtains and blinds when showing your home. Add supplemental lighting where necessary. Outdated or broken light fixtures can be cheaply and easily replaced. If you think your existing fixtures are fine, make sure to dust them, clean off any grime and empty out the dead bugs.

Furniture

Craft your product. Regardless of your feelings, people want to see a happy setting. Light up your tears and act as if the person behind the mask has everything under control. Furnish your life with light colors to declutter any heaviness. Make sure furniture is the right size for the room, and do not clutter a room with too much furniture. Furniture that is too big will make a room look small, while too little or too small furniture can make a space feel cold. You will also want to arrange the furniture in a way that makes each room feel spacious, yet homey. In the living room, for example, seating should be set up in a way that creates a gathering area around the fireplace.

Walls and Ceilings

Plaster the structures as if there is no fissures and crevices that could show weakness. Cracks in the walls or ceiling are a red flag to buyers as they may indicate foundation problems. If your home does have foundation problems, you will need to either fix them or alert potential buyers to the problem. That said, a fix would be better in terms of getting the home sold. If the foundation only looks bad, but has been deemed sound by an inspector, repair the cracks so you do not scare off buyers.

Exterior

Esthetic appearance is the first card you show when you want to sell. Your home's exterior will be the first impression buyers get and may even determine their interest in viewing the inside. Make sure your lawn, hedges, trees and other plants are well maintained and neatly pruned and eliminate any weeds. To brighten windows, wash them well, and consider adding flower boxes to brighten them up further. If you can, power wash your home's exterior – it can make it look almost freshly painted but with less effort and expense. Make sure the sidewalk leading up to the house is clear and clean, and purchase new doormats for the front and back doors.

Last Touches

Just before any open house or showing, make sure that your staging efforts go the full mile with a few last-minute touches that will make the home seem warm and inviting. These include fresh flowers, letting fresh air into the house for at least ten minutes beforehand so it is not stuffy, adding a pleasant scent as discussed earlier, and putting new, plush, nicely folded towels in the bathrooms.

Bottom Line

You want to emphasize the home's best features, but keep in mind that what sells the home and what will make the home usable for the buyer are not necessarily the same thing.

I got it! Staging a home is like staging your life. You cherished your place for some years and collected memories. You look for the next step, next adventure, next challenge, next opportunity and you move on. If things are not so clean, meaning if there are unfinished conversations, lack of honest dialogue, "stains" in relationships, you clean them, to move onto the next step without carrying the dirt, the filth, with you. Do not try to evade the conversation that might be uncomfortable at the time. Good communication is necessary for the positive outcome in conflict resolution.

You look at the walls and the ceilings, the interior as well as the exterior. Do not clutter the grime because at the end of the day it shows and it might even stink.

If the foundations of those relationships are broken, fix them. They will not be fixed miraculously by an external force. It will only happen if you fix them; otherwise they will break deeper and deeper until the walls collapse.

Ask yourself: Am I taking good care of my life, the one I received as a gift? Do I preserve in good standards my internal features as much as I care for my external features? Do I take good care of the ones I love? Do I spend quality time with them? Have I said "I love you" enough times and at the right time so I do not regret it if it happens to be too late? Did I asked for forgiveness, when, knowingly or unaware, I committed a mistake and I hurt someone?

Lightning? Bring light and understanding into your life. Nurture your soul, stimulate your intellect, and start something new. Do not get too comfortable in your own skin. Do not get bored; it is dangerous. There is so much to explore, to discover, to share, and to enjoy.

Let me share a letter I wrote to my home:

Dear Home,

Thank you! You welcomed us into your walls. You showed yourself just the way you are. I fell in love with you. I knew you were the right one since the first moment I passed by you. We filled you with sounds and noise, with serenity and calmness, with joy and tears, and you never complained. You embraced every moment and made for us a home.

We saw our beautiful girls grow into amazing women, celebrating ritual milestones, accomplishments and graduations and your walls whispered, "Congratulations! Mazal Tov!" We received friends from all over the world, and you understood their languages because they spoke the universal language of friendship, love and memories. You heard music and danced with us. You allowed us to see our family and community blossom. You allowed us to celebrate weddings in your gorgeous basement and to tutor children in their journey to adulthood. You allowed us to distribute invitations to celebrate holidays and to teach Talmud classes at 7 AM and Kabballah courses at 9PM. The home that never sleeps...thank you.

Beloved home, thank you for being so discrete, for keeping the secrets of those who came to share their feelings, those who cried and those who laughed. Thank you for expanding your walls to fit more people for Shabbat dinners and at the end of Shabbat, for lighting up with a braided candle and perfuming yourself with aromatic spices. Thank you for allowing us, in the month that leads to Passover, to look for every fermented piece of food and diligently clean every corner and surface.

Today is a big day, the Mezuzah--Jewish symbol at the entrance of the gates and doors-- that we affixed on your walls on August 10, 2003, is moving with us. Tears roll down my face. You are the first home we ever bought and we are not abandoning you. We are treasuring every memory, and we hope that whoever gets you next will love you as much as we did, will appreciate your beauty and comfort, and will enjoy your welcoming attitude.

*Thank you for being just that… our **home**.*

With love, profound gratitude and respect,
Your dweller and seeker, Analia

I ask myself, what are the "real" non-staged memories we carry in life? How do you stage those memories? Can we even stage those memories?

YOUR PERSONAL CONTEMPLATION

$\mathscr{Six}$

FEARS

"Be patient toward all that is unsolved in your heart and to try to love the questions themselves like locked rooms and like books that are written in a very foreign tongue."

Rainer Maria Rilke (1875-1926)

In our daily life, we often bring timeless characters that inspire us and give us hope. Based on their experiences, we look at our lives through different lenses. Based on their results, we craft our paths in different ways. Even though I rarely read blogs, I did come across this entry by Jenni written on May 18 2011, <u>Struggling with Uncertainty</u>:

> *"I never liked gambling because I hate taking risks. The expected return is never guaranteed. Similarly, in life, there are just so many uncontrollable risks that people take on, filled with feelings of uncertainty, fear which sometimes, if not always, leaves us all with a sense of loss. How can we cope with these feelings of uncertainty? Especially when there are no guaranteed results? Or what's even more troublesome, if the results*

78

are never as we expect? However, if we never take that risk, when will one ever know if they win or lose? And if that window of opportunity shuts down, would feelings of regret be worse?"

Carl Sagan in his infinite wisdom taught:

"The chief deficiency I see in the skeptical movement is in its polarization: Us vs Them--the sense that we have a monopoly on the truth; that those other people who believe in all these stupid doctrines are morons; that if you are sensible, you will listen to us; and if not; you are beyond redemption. This is unconstructive...whereas, a compassionate approach that from the beginning acknowledges that human roots of pseudoscience and superstition might be much more widely accepted. If we understand this, then of course we feel the uncertainty and pain of the abductees, or those who dare not leave home without consulting their horoscopes, or those who pin their hopes on crystals from Atlantis."

Often, our fears and anxieties find an escaping path through anchors of certainty based on a cosmic openness that broadens our horizons. We live in a permanent hunt for certainty and thrive for its presence but life is about uncertainties.

Rainer Maria Rilke writes:

"I want to beg you, as much as I can, dear sir, to be patient toward all that is unsolved in your heart and to try to love the questions themselves like locked rooms and like books that are written in a very foreign tongue. Do not now seek the answers, which cannot be given you because you would not be able to live them. And the point is, to live everything. Live the questions now.

Perhaps you will then gradually, without noticing it,
live along some distant day into the answer."

Rilke exhorted us to live with questions and instead of looking for the certainty in answer, to dare to formulate more questions in the endless labyrinth of discoveries.

Rilke's invitation to dive in the ocean of uncertainty opposed John Dewey's approach to <u>The Quest for Certainty</u>: *"If a man could not conquer destiny, he could willingly ally himself with it; putting his will, even in sore affliction, on the side of the powers which dispense fortune, he could escape defeat and might triumph in the midst of destruction" (Gifford Lectures, 1929).*

Some of us carry a fixation for the need of certainty, and need to be reassured that the fate-destiny-future presented to us will have a good outcome. Others live with the game of uncertainty and it is in this scenario that find the joy of freedom, spiritual drive and peace of mind.

Evolution showed us that although natural selection does happen, many factors, conditions and environmental considerations could change the course of our paths and the destiny of ourselves. In the words of Darwin:

> *"If during the long course of ages and under varying conditions of life, organic beings vary at all in their several parts of their organization, and I think this cannot be disputed; if there be, owing to the high geometrical powers of increase of each species, at some age, season, or year, a severe struggle for life, and this certainly cannot be disputed, then, considering the infinite complexity of the relations of all organic beings to each other and to their conditions of existence, causing an infinite diversity in structure, constitution and habits, to be adventurous to them, I think it would a most extraordinary fact if no variation ever*

*had occurred useful to each being own welfare…this
principle of preservation, I have called for the sake of
brevity, Natural Selection.*

(Darwin, Origin of Species, 1859)

Is this natural selection a source of concern? Does it add to the
fears that might overcome our being? Are these fears paralyzing us?
Are these fears detracting us from functioning? Anxiety generated
from fear often impedes people from acting.

I love scuba diving. As a diver, I'm able to discover a magnificent
world that otherwise would be concealed to me. The plentiful diverse
community in the ocean as well as the dance of the corals and algae,
energizes me and enhances my spiritual awareness of God's creation.
I depend on an oxygen tank, physiological knowledge, and the trust
and confidence that everything will go well. A leap of faith helps
as well.

On the other hand, I'm afraid of heights. Uncontrollable
palpitations invade my body every time I need to drive on a bridge.

Fears. When I lost my voice, I needed to conquer the fear of
silence. Silence may disguise aloneness or can open the endless
possibilities of the encounter with God, self, the fellow human, the
world. **The fear of silence is an invitation to contemplate.**

Overcoming the fears of uncertainty, reinforce our willingness
to explore and expose mistakes that help us to grow.

> *"If one wants to be active, one mustn't be afraid to do
> something wrong sometimes, not afraid to lapse into
> some mistakes. You don't know how paralyzing it is,
> that stare from a blank canvas that says to the painter you
> can't do anything. The canvas has an idiotic stare,
> and mesmerizes some painters so that they turn into
> idiots themselves. Many painters are afraid of the
> blank canvas, but the blank canvas IS AFRAID of*

the truly passionate painter who dares — and who has once broken the spell of "you can't." Life itself likewise always turns towards one an infinitely meaningless, discouraging, dispiriting blank side on which there is nothing, any more than on a blank canvas."

(Vincent Van Gogh, Letter to Theo, 1884)

YOUR PERSONAL CONTEMPLATION

Seven

ACCEPTANCE

"Doubt is not a pleasant condition, but certainty, is an absurd one."

François-Marie Arouet-*Voltaire (1694-1778)*

My favorite Talmudic story is found in *Baba Metziah* 59 b. It is a very well-known story about the discussion between Rabbis regarding an oven that belonged to a fellow called *Achnai*. The focus of the story is mostly about the centrality of argument and the acceptance, or not, of the other's opinion.

> *One day, Rabbi Joshua and Rabbi Eliezer were having a legal argument over the purity of the oven of Achnai. Rabbi Eliezer brought them evidence to legitimize his opinion but Rabbi Joshua rejected him. Upon being disallowed, Rabbi Eliezer said to Rabbi Joshua, "if the law is with me, then let the carob tree prove it!" to which the carob tree uprooted itself and moved one hundred cubits--some say four hundred cubits. Rabbi Joshua responded by saying that one cannot prove anything from a carob tree.*

Rabbi Eliezer then said to him, "then if the law is with me, let the stream prove it!" to which the water of the stream responded by flowing in the opposite direction. Rabbi Joshua responded by saying that one cannot prove anything with a stream.

Rabbi Eliezer then said, "if the law is with me, let the walls of the house of study prove it!" to which the walls of the room began to incline. Rabbi Joshua then rebuke the walls by saying that the walls have no authority in a legal debate. The walls then stood at angles, tilted, in respect to both Rabbis.

Finally, Rabbi Eliezer said "if the law is with me, then may it be proven by heaven!". In response to this, a voice came down from heaven and said to Rabbi Joshua, "why do you argue with Rabbi Eliezer? The law is in accordance with him in every way." Rabbi Joshua said to the heavenly voices, THE TORAH IS NOT IN HEAVEN (Deuteronomy 30:12). What did God say to that exclamation? God said with delight "My children have defeated me; my children have defeated me".

It is certainly a mesmerizing piece of Talmudic discussion, intellectual dissertation and control—the power of the law, that once given at Sinai, was crafted in the hands of the Rabbis. Is there acceptance on the side of the Rabbis? Do they embrace the opinion of each other or is game a competing point, a way of embarrassing those who are losing power? What's God's reaction?

The reason I consider this text a phenomenal tool for learning, resides in God's answer. "My children have defeated me--*Nitzchuni Banai*" The root of the word *nitzchuni* N-TZ-CH, has different meanings. The most popular translation is victory (*Nitzachon*), but I like to read it in a different way, NETZACH=ETERNITY. God is saying, through your discussion, you are bringing Me to eternity. You maintain Me alive so long as there is dialogue, arguments, and you do not just dwell in conformity. You maintain ME when you SEEK for new answers.

The truth is that the story does not have a happy ending. Rabbi Eliezer is ostracized and, through curses and vile anger, another Rabbi dies.

Often, human beings struggle with the capacity of maintaining a civilized discourse, embracing others' opinions and respecting them. In the interaction of dissent, Rabbi Nathan Lopes Cardozo writes:

> *"Criticism should not be quarrelsome and destructive, but should rather be guiding, instructive and inspiring. Judaism has never feared dissent and debate but has in fact encouraged it. What, after all, is the benefit of condemnation if Judaism simultaneously loses its soul?"*

> (Rabbinical Tyranny and
> Freedom of Thought- January 18, 2017)

There is an empowering sense of possession of The Truth, as if there would only be one truth. In the path of acceptance, French philosopher and Holocaust survivor, Emmanuel Levinas derived the prevalence of his ethics and the way he sees the universe of relationships in the experience of the encounter with the Other. The Other deserves a capital "O". For Levinas, the irreducible relation, the epiphany, of the face-to-face, the encounter with another, is an honored occurrence in which the other person's proximity and distance are both strongly felt. It is in that presence that the natural separation of the Self enables the consideration of the distinguished persona. "The Other precisely reveals himself in his alterity not in a shock negating the I, but as the primordial phenomenon of gentleness."

One instantly recognizes the transcendence and heteronomy of the Other. Acceptance is about the celebration of similarities and the embrace of differences. Acceptance is defeating our sealed mental understanding and allowing our boundaries to expand. Acceptance is unplugging the cables of thought control. Acceptance is about conquering our arrogance in thinking that we have the only answer. Acceptance is growth, expansion, progress, and evolution.

YOUR PERSONAL CONTEMPLATION

MEMORIES

I would simply like to reclaim an old and, alas, quite unfashionable private formula: Moderate enjoyment is double enjoyment. And: Do not overlook the little joys!

(Hermann Hesse 1877-1962)

STOP AND SMELL THE FLOWERS.

Soren Kierkegaard scolded in 1843: *"Of all ridiculous things the most ridiculous seems to me, to be busy — to be a man who is brisk about his food and his work"*, as he described our greater source of unhappiness.

One of the most difficult tasks in our daily routine is to find balance. We find ourselves juggling our various obligations, between needs and being needed, to please ourselves and please others, to give and to receive. Balance between our time INVESTED in personal relationships, professional obligations, enjoyments of leisure, hobbies, etc. The list could be long and the stress added to the fulfilment of the "checklist" could become overwhelming. Sometimes we pretend to add to this list since it is also important to show to ourselves that we are busy. That makes us feel "valuable".

In the Hebrew language, balance (*izzun*) and ear (*ozzen*) have the same root. As we know from neuroanatomy and neurophysiology, the vestibulocochlear nerve is responsible for the sense of hearing and it is also pertinent to balance, to the body position sense. Should we listen to our body-soul connection to find balance?

The Greek philosophers emphasize the importance of contemplation as a basis of free thinking. Unplugging from the demanding routine allowed them to expand their knowledge of the course of life. Similarly, John Locke (1632-1704) wrote on his composition entitled "An Essay Concerning Human Understanding": *Let us then suppose the mind to be, as we say, white paper void of all characters, without any ideas. How comes it to be furnished? Whence comes it by that vast store which the busy and boundless fancy of man has painted on it an almost endless variety? When has it all the materials of reason and knowledge? To this I answer, in one word, from EXPERIENCE.*

Experiences create memories. Many of them we leave a deep imprint throughout life. Memories are enigmatic. How does our brain store and filter memories? Which mechanism do we use to sift what we want to remember? Can we, even, choose them? Memories are crafted throughout time, but they are not staged; they reflect real life and they mirror real relationships.

I started writing this book a year after the death of my beloved father--on his *Yortzait* (*yor*-year/ *tzait*- time).

One of the most meaningful moments of my life happened to me on June, 2013. My dad was dying surrounded by his family-- the people he loved the most. There was a sense of Holiness in the room. That afternoon I asked my dad, "Would you like me to sing you a song?" He answered, "Yes." I expected he would ask for a Tango lyric, but not this time. He said, *"Avinu Malkeynu"* -- a traditional prayer of our liturgy that we chant during the Days of Awe, High Holidays, asking God to inscribe and seal us in the book of a good quality of life. So, I started singing *Avinu Malkeyinu*... Our Father our King answer us, have compassion on us. My dad was a *MENTSCH*, a good person, with all capital letters and had no unfinished business.

He asked for forgiveness at the right time. He had an amazing memory and did not forget anything, but he had the ability to move on even when he had been hurt. So, the time came when I opened the window to say the *Vidui,* the last confession, the same one that we do at the end of Yom Kippur and I turned around and he recited the *Shemah Israel* as his last words, and then he added some words that were hard to be heard. In his last stream of strength, he whispered:

She'Echeyanu V'Kyimanu v'Yiguianu laZman HaZe
[Blessed are You... Who have sustained us with life, gave us our existence and allow us to live this moment].

Holding hands with his life partner, my mom, he died *shalem-*WHOLE and with holiness.

Three years later, my mom died. This time she was not holding hands with the love of her life, but she died in exactly the same hospital room as my father. She missed him very much. They had lived together over half a century and they walked throughout life respecting each other's pace and swinging their own dance.

Several times a week I like to play a game when I am by myself. I like to "Unfreeze Photographs." Have you ever done that? Let's play the game. Let me show you this. It is just a picture. Judging by it sepia color and the fact that no one is smiling, it is probably an old one. And yes, it is. What if I unfroze a photo and let it talk many years later? What do you see? How many secrets are hidden behind? How many visions became reality and how many dreams were doomed in the unfulfilled file?

While my mom was hospitalized I sat for hours next to her. She helped me unfreeze hundreds of pictures that recall multiple stories of life and death--beautiful memories. I wrote each name on the back of the photograph and reconstructed my family album. The ones from Europe and the ones for the Jewish holidays. First *Rosh*

HaShannah or Passover *Seder* celebrated in Argentina, for those who were able to escape from the Nazis in Europe.

I felt the piercing presence of the absence. Mami-my mom-walked me for a long time, the first steps, the first training wheels of the bike, the first big decision (and many more afterwards), the first call on my birthdays...a firm walk, with elegance, confidence, dignity, always sealed with a Shem Tov, a good name. Then, I started walking her, holding hands, trying to find the perfect balance. I miss and will miss the daily calls that would always start by saying "I was just thinking of you." Apparently, she was always thinking of me.

That's the piercing presence of the absence.

Rabbi Bradley Artson, nails the concept of relational-holiness: "Just as light can only be seen when it bounces off a physical object, so too holiness (*kedushah*) can only be shared and encountered when it is embodied in social and communal structures." We treasure those moments of holiness in life by making the ordinary become extraordinary-- sanctifying the present as a gift we renew every day. Memories, even the good ones, and their sense of loss teach that life is unpredictable and that the meritocrat's efforts at total control are an illusion. That pain instilled by loss, oddly, also teaches gratitude. For the moments, even those short moments of happiness, gifted by the presence.

People may start their suffering asking "Why me?" or "Why evil?" But they soon realize the proper question is, "What am I supposed to do if I am confronted with suffering, if I am the victim of evil?" Recovering from suffering is not like recovering from a disease. Many people do not come out healed; they come out different. They crash through the logic of individual utility and behave paradoxically. Instead of recoiling from the sorts of loving commitments that often lead to suffering, they throw themselves more deeply into them. Even while experiencing the worst and most lacerating consequences, some people double down on vulnerability and become available to healing love. They hurl themselves deeper and more gratefully into their art, loved ones, and commitments.

Let me share a personal experience. I left my home in the suburbs of Buenos Aires the day I got married. It was one of the most joyous occasions of my life. My dad and my mom walked me to my wedding canopy where I started a beautiful journey along with my best friend. Around the kitchen table, for many years, my family gathered together. We laughed a lot, we shared our secrets, we celebrated success, and we studied piles of books. And those books adorned that kitchen, that desk, that table. We lit Shabbat candles, filled with charitable coins the *tzedakah* box, we sorted samples of pharmaceutical companies to distribute to the poor every Sunday, and we introduced our boyfriend(s) and girlfriends (candidates needed to be approved, first by my *Zeide*-grandfather, then Papi-dad- and after being scrutinized, Mami-mom- gave they final endorsement (sometimes...).

Once married, it was around that same table that my brothers and I announced the coming of grandchildren. It was then that my parents decided to slow down, think of retirement and follow us (actually the grandchildren) all over the world. No birthday party, talent show, endless dance recital, special awards' ceremony, ritual milestones or graduations has ever been missed. *Papi & Mami* were ALWAYS present, ALWAYS. There are some people who could live geographically close and be distant, and there are others in which distance is only an opportunity to become even closer and enjoy the real important moments of life.

That morning, as I walked through the familiar streets that know my steps and saw me grow, memories and tears embraced my soul. I walked to the hospital where both my parents were treated like royalty (both died in the same hospital they helped found). I brought some gifts to the doctors, nurses and other staff and thanked them for their compassion, love, dedication and professional expertise (lots of love and dedication in the Argentinean doctors) and left, knowing that probably after so many times this will be my last visit. I went to my childhood elementary school and my synagogue. I said goodbye and thanked them for years of fun and learning, and for planting strong Zionist roots that matched my parents' love for Israel.

Back home, I packed letters, our daughters' first small shoes, a prayer book with a dried orchid inside, pictures, pictures, pictures, and thousands of pictures. I packed my grandfather's cane, that my dad and mom used later in life. I closed each closet, smelled each smell, cried each cry, closed windows and curtains. Kissed the clothes that will be donated, turned off the lights, unplugged the phone and, with an aching heart and an absolutely confused mind, as if I am leaving in a completely different dimension with an out of body experience, I kissed the *mezuzah* one last time and left. I left behind the keys of my early years... How do you pack your childhood and teen age years in two suitcases?

At the Delta counter in Buenos Aires, Argentina, my two pieces of luggage were overweight. The woman looked at me and said, "You will have to pay for the weight excess." I responded, "How do you put a price to values that are priceless?" She asked me what was I carrying and I said "**my childhood**, now that both mom and dad are gone, I can only carry my childhood alone." She also cried and let me go.

Memories are the unfrozen photographs of treasuring life, a gift. A gift of our loved ones and their passing throughout our lives, and the impact they have made has been inscribed in our heart, minds, souls and actions. I miss that "every day call." I miss the other side telling me, "I was just thinking of you." But I celebrate those memories and craft them, and shower them with love and harmony.

My parents remain alive through these memories.

May their memories be for blessings. AMEN.

YOUR PERSONAL CONTEMPLATION

Nine

TRANSCENDENCE

"Success is not final, failure is not fatal, it is the courage to continue that counts."

Winston Churchill (1874-1965)

Street photography is wordless and communicates a lot.

An eye for the beauty of life through lenses of penetration. They capture the beauty of life as it is-- in pure form. Myopic minds blind our ability to watch, see, and observe. Blindness that obscures our capacity of discoveries erases possible new horizons. When Alfred Eisenstaedt captured the famous kiss at Times Square on V-J Day, he probably did not know that that picture would capture the joy of that glorious day as an icon for posterity. That picture is protected by copyright, nevertheless when I mention the photo we all know the image.

The opportunity to transcend is presented on regular basis and, often, when we do not expect it. The implications of our daily behaviors, some of which we consider simple and, might leave a profound impact on other people's lives. It is that moment, that picture, that kiss, that right word at the right time, that can build or destroy a whole world. That is how we transcend.

I experienced transcendence on a Thursday night, September 25, 2008, in room 682 at Piedmont Hospital, in Atlanta, Georgia. My husband and I went to say good bye to a young dear friend. We all knew he was dying and this was our last chance to visit with him.

The three of us held hands and shared twenty-five minutes of special time in the "togetherness" that connect us in those unique moments, luminal thresholds between life and death. In this triangle of friendship and love, we recalled sweet tears of memories as we evoked our friendship of eight years. During our time alone, I asked, "Sam, do you fear anything?"

Sam was one of the most intelligent, self-driven, and tireless people I have ever met. I thought he understood that I was referring to the afterlife and his encounter with God. But Sam answered, "I fear and wonder if my family will be OK." The generosity of his failing heart did not stop even at the end. There was no reason for him to fear his pending encounter with God. He knew that not only would he be good company to God, but he would also help organize things up there, so the Earth could be a better place. Nevertheless, his worry was about his loved ones, simply because love transcends even the enigma of death.

While some of us were blessed to have the opportunity to say good bye, sometimes…sometimes…there is no chance to say good bye. At those moments, our feelings are a mixture of sorrow, anger, shame, and distress and we often ask, WHY? Why did she/he do this to me? The fact is our loved ones do not die to hurt us, but their loss is a painful burden we bear.

At funerals, we do not focus on how our loved ones died, but on how they lived – how they celebrated life. Eric Shurenberg, managing editor of Money Magazine began his October 2008 column with the following statement: "If you watched the Jamaican sprinter Usian Bolt at the Beijing Olympics, you know there are 2 ways to close out a race. You can ease off and start to celebrate before you quite get to the finish line, as Bolt did in his 100-meter final, or you can put your head down and drive hard all the way through the homestretch, as he did in the 200." Bolt won both ways. Shurenberg used this theme to look at retirement strategies, pointing out that as you near the finish line at the end of your working years, it is important to follow the hard-charging strategy.

So, what is the hard charging strategy? The way we live our lives every day. Our appreciation of every moment. And our plans for a better future – that is the hard charging strategy. We have seen this message in the words of great thinkers throughout the ages. Horace wrote, "Carpe diem"—seize the day-- take advantage of every moment in life and live it with intensity. Set your priorities.

Bahya ibn Pakuda, a Sephardic medieval thinker, said "our days are like scrolls, write on them what you want to be remembered for." I would add to his proclamation "Live to the fullest, so YOU can be present, and that will manifest your transcendence." There are certain moments in life when at a large gathering of people, we should ask ourselves: "Although we are ALL here, together, where is each one of us?" Though we are in the same place at the same time, each of us comes with a personal agenda, our own dreams, fears, hopes, hurts and memories. Each of us is an incomplete, unfulfilled person in some way. Some of us have been left incomplete by death, some by divorce, and some by fear. Many of us are left with disappointments-- the job we wanted but didn't get; the talent we believed would have made us happy, but never managed to develop; or the child that didn't turn out as we hoped he would. Our incompleteness drives us. Our losses and missing pieces compel us to see everything in our lives through a unique lens.

According to the *Hassidic* Master, the Kotzker *Rebbe* "There is nothing in the world as whole as a broken heart." People may ask: "Rabbi, where was God when I lost my best friend? Where was God during this ecological disaster? Where was God when my kids' college fund or my retirement money melted in the hot furnace of Wall Street?" Well, Judaism does not believe in the God of happy endings, but rather in the God who takes you by the hand and leads you THROUGH the valley of the shadow of death so that you do not have to spend the rest of your life IN the valley, in darkness. In this way, you come to know a God who will help people live meaningful lives even without the happy endings, and a God who teaches wisdom and fortitude, so that people can find beauty and courage in the stories of their lives, no matter how they end.

There is a story told of two Buddhist monks making a pilgrimage to a shrine in India. As they are traveling they come to a mud lake, and they see an attractive young girl in a beautiful new dress standing by the edge of the lake afraid to cross for fear of ruining her dress. One of the monks impulsively picks her up and carries her across the puddle. The second monk is put off by what his friend did, and for the rest of the day it bothers him. He does not say much to his friend; he almost stops talking to him. Finally, at the day's end, when they stop to cook for dinner, he says to his companion, "You know, it's not right for people like us to get too close to women. They represent temptation and we are monks! His friend turned to him and said: "Are you STILL carrying that girl? I put her down six hours ago."

We are carrying burdens of bitter memories and resentments, and we cannot imagine the sense of relief and freedom we would feel when we find the courage to put those burdens down.

As I am writing this book, there are many companies developing virtual reality technology. People can use sensors on helmets and gloves to experience a different setting in life through computer-generated simulations. The consumer can climb Mount Everest, dive in the ocean, float in space, enter a Japanese ryokan, or simply be part of everyday life. The accelerating occurrence is tempting clients to detach themselves from their own reality and transcend into a world of algorithms that present a desired (sometimes not so much desired) space and time. It is an interesting concept and certainly a colossal advance in the world of science if these machines could be used to treat phobias, paranoias, or any kind of mental and psychosomatic diseases.

We compose every day our virtual machine and then we experience its reality as we walk through the program. We are those algorithms. Our uniqueness and individuality creates a customized machine that appreciates our own being and decodes transcendence.

YOUR PERSONAL CONTEMPLATION

Ten

ETHICAL WILL

The future belongs to those who believe in the beauty of their dreams.

Anna Eleanor Roosevelt (1884-1962)

Have you signed your will? Have you chosen your proxy? Have you expressed your end of life wishes? Advanced directives of how/when/why/what/ you need in the final moments of your life. Do Not Resuscitate-DNR? Allow Natural Death-AND? How about your estate?

I wrote my Ethical Will. That is my legacy-- my gift to my children. Eighteen items I would like them to carry for the rest of their lives and to, hopefully, serve as an inspiration for them, to write their own and pass it to the next generation. Why eighteen? Because the numerical Hebrew value of eighteen is composed with the letters that explicit the word *CHAI*-LIFE. This is my heritage.

1. **A Tree: with strong roots and strong branches to know where are we coming from and to embrace the universe.**

2. Wings: to defy gravity, spread them wide and fly.

3. A Map: To explore the world and see its beauty

4. A Magnifier: To see the splendor in the smallest aspects of life.

5. A Clock: To make every second count and live it to the fullest.

6. A Blank notebook: To inscribe adventures.

7. A question mark: To never lose the capacity to ask.

8. An exclamation mark: inviting Awareness: To see awe, make a new blessing and treasure God's presence.

9. Comfortable shoes: To walk your OWN unique walk.

10. A megaphone: To speak up for those who are silenced and be heard clearly.

11. A pillow: To RELAX and contemplate that the universe is big and there is so much to be discovered.

12. A Maze: To explore different paths, those will guide you to transformative wisdom.

13. A book: To dive into the ocean of knowledge and expose you to think.

14. A hiking stick: To feel safe through steps of self-confidence.

15. A blanket: To host warmth.

16. Sunglasses: To have FUN.

17. A scale: To balance your actions.

18. A tridimensional mirror: To esteem your inside beauty and see beauty in others.

Disclaimer: Readers, the different font and the extra space in between lines of this ethical will, is for YOU to add your personal notes and/or to rewrite your own will.

"Count the number of achievements you have had in your life, then count the number of dreams you have for life, as long as the number of your dreams is greater than your achievements, you will stay young"

Shimon Peres,
President of the State of Israel. 1923-2016

YOUR PERSONAL CONTEMPLATION

EPILOGUE AND
THE ART OF FINDING BALANCE

"Somewhere something incredible is waiting for us"

Carl Sagan (1934-1986)

Bob Eidelstein, L.M.F.T, posted on January 31 2012 in Psychology Today,

> *"Paying attention to the silence as the space between our verbal exchanges allows the meaning of these exchanges to be assimilated into our psyches and from that place of depth, our creative engagement naturally flows. Creative engagement with our internal processes allows us to discover more of who we are, to take in previously hidden aspects of ourselves, and to reconfigure ourselves, if we so choose. This is what allows us to be more deeply authentic in the present moment. By being more authentic, we become more self-actualized and can impact our world in powerful ways."*

Paying attention to the silence between spaces and creating those spaces to emit a sound are the characteristics of one of my favorite instruments, the *Shofar*—ram's horn. The Shofar was used in biblical times to call the community both for celebration and for war, to announce holidays, and to congregate before battle. The community comes together at the sound of the Shofar. Everyone carrying their own expectations and anxieties. Everyone responding to the call of the Shofar.

Shofar comes from the Hebrew root, SH P R, *leshaper,* meaning to improve, to advance, to increase, to mend, to progress, or to expand. The sound of the Shofar and the silence in between represent both construction and devastation. The Shofar is a symbol of our lives. Through the different reverberations, it calls us for comfort and uneasiness.

Rabbi Bradley Artson explains: *"Just as light can only be seen when it bounces off a physical object, so too holiness (kedushah) can only be shared and encountered when it is embodied in social and communal structures."* We treasure those moments of holiness in life by making the ordinary become extraordinary-- sanctifying the present as a gift we renew every day.

In the prayer book for the High Holidays, Mahzor Hadash- page 248, an adaptation has been made from the words of Milton Steinberg, about the Shofar. Let me quote some excerpts:

Tekiah: The ongoing sound. Awake! Let not habit dull your minds, nor comfort harden your hearts. Examine your deeds, look well into your soul, mend your ways...As we hear the sharp Tekiah blast, let us rouse ourselves from smugness and self-satisfaction, from callousness and self-righteousness.

Shevarim: These three discontinuous blasts, are broken sounds. They are like a staccato cry. They beg for attention, or maybe for mercy. *Shevarim* is a call to action, to listen to the oppressed and the neglected. *Shevarim* is that call to action. To walk the walk.

Teruah: In nine pieces that sound breaks. Enough, how much longer can we hold it? Are we carrying those broken tablets as they become heavier, unbearable? Only from this broken-shattered piece we can build wholeness again.

Tekiah Gedolah: The uninterrupted, pristine sound. It collects the pieces of the broken melodies and magically transports us into perfection. Unblemished, immaculate, this sound elevates our spirit and gives us hope.

Why do I mention the sounds of the Shofar? The broken pieces and the in crescendo composition are modes to approach life. I dedicated this book to the strength and lessons I learned from a young man, Zack. This is, partially, his story. A story that defined my relationship with him, but does NOT define him.

Tekiah

His name is Zack; I met him several years ago, a 19-year-old at the time, a college student from Massachusetts. He came back from a summer program visiting Israel and was hired as a counselor in a camp in Maine.

Shevarim

July 12, 2005, is Zack's day off at camp. He decides that is a good day to go canoeing with his friends. He jumps from the canoe, in a shallow place, and hits his back. My friend and colleague, the Rabbi of Zack's family's congregation in Needhan, MA, tells me the story. Zack will be taken care of in Atlanta, at the Shepherd Center, just thirty minutes from our home. At that moment, I felt, it was another tragic story, I did not know that that story will change my life.

T'rua

Cervical 2? 3? 4? Diagnosis quadriplegia; prognosis electric wheelchair; time uncertain, probably forever. *Itzchak ben Adina*, that's Zack's Hebrew name. Like Isaac, the biblical character, he is bound, not to the altar but to the chair.

I visited Zack throughout a year. I met his incredible-compassionate and strong parents, Elliot and Adrianne, and his best cheerleader, sister, Danielle. Zack changed my life. Anonymously, without knowing it, he had an incredible capacity for transforming people's lives. Not just because he IS an actor, but because of his determination he did not need to STAGE and craft his life to sell the story of struggle. He showed a different view of this quote from "The Little Prince": "I have to put up with two or three caterpillars if I want to get to know the butterflies."

Since the day I met him, every single day of my life, for over eleven years, at the time of writing this book, Zack has been in my thoughts. Every. Single. Day. Without exception. According to the Hassidic Master, the Kotzker Rebbe: "There is nothing in the world as whole as a broken heart."

Tekiah Gedolah:

The continuous sound of the Shofar, the uninterrupted notes of defiance, crown this melody. Zack is today married to his angel-wife and the proud father of a boy. Zack is a miracle maker.

Since July 29, 2005, the day I met Zack, I learned that the sky is the limit. You can be a great dancer without moving your legs, and you can be an inspiring theatre playwright without moving your hand ...yet.

We hear the sounds of the Shofar– the ram's horn that substituted for Isaac, at his binding. The sounds of the piercing silence, the broken tablets, the fears that paralyze us, the memories that cherish blasts and muteness, the acceptance of coping with life difficulties and unfulfilled dreams.

The 16th century Kabbalistic work, *Reshit Chochmah,* teaches that the Ark, where the scrolls of Torah reside, is a symbol of the human heart and Brokenness and Wholeness coexist side by side in the chambers of the heart.

We celebrate through pristine melodies the permanent awareness of miracles that surround us, that make us transcend, that expose us to fragility and strengthen us with understanding, crafting and staging our inner-self with a mysterious enchantment of life's joy. So, whenever we look at the light through tears of pain, we can see the colors of the rainbow, liberating ourselves from enslaving habits and embracing those shattered pieces of our memorabilia.

I started writing this book at the one year anniversary of the death of my father and I finish it on the one year anniversary of the death of my mother. Two soulmates who are dancing in heaven, who inspired me and taught me that not even the sky is the limit. So, I flew.

Printed in the United States
By Bookmasters